TEACHING
TOTAL
PERCUSSION

Kenneth A. Mueller

Teaching
Total
Percussion

Parker Publishing Company, Inc.
West Nyack, N. Y.

Printed in the United States of America
ISBN-0-13-895953-6
B & P

Dedication

To Gordon Peters for introducing the
idea of total percussion to me and
his inspiration to improve percussion education; and
To my wife, Judy, for her many hours
of help and understanding.

The How and Why of Teaching Total Percussion

This book is written for the high school instrumental music educator. Through its use he will gain insight into the concepts of teaching total percussion. By total percussion, I am referring to the training of students to play, with equal ability, in the three major areas of percussion: snare drum, timpani and the mallet percussion instruments. It also implies that the student be trained to play any of the vast amount of "accessory" percussion instruments correctly and with competence.

This book shows how to teach all of the percussion instruments through an understanding of their relationship to each other. You will find important facts about each percussion instrument, an explanation of how to teach each of these and, more important, how to coordinate this instruction so that you may begin to develop students well versed in the total area of percussion. Also, you will learn how to develop an effective total percussion program that can fit into your established band or orchestra program. Special emphasis will be given to the development of an effective and interesting marching percussion section and the development of a percussion ensemble to help in total percussion training.

In addition, this book will provide you with much practical information needed when you begin to teach total percussion such as: equipping the percussion section for total percussion education, taking care of percussion equipment, and guidelines in the selection of literature and the creation of instructional materials needed in teaching total percussion.

Through its use this book will help you train percussion students so that they will develop into good musicians, with a mature control of the total percussion area, and the ability to play in a musical manner any and all percussion music they receive as a part of the band program. Composers of contemporary music are acknowledging and understanding the wide range of sound available through percussion. Thus, modern band music is generally much more demanding of the percussion section. How difficult it is for the band director to teach and direct such works if his percussionists do not know how to play all of the percussion instruments!

Nor should percussion students be prevented from pursuing a career in music education and/or applied percussion if they so desire and have the ability. Yet, in today's music field there is little room for the person who specializes on one percussion instrument. The college which accepts a percussion major who cannot play reasonably well in the areas of snare drum, timpani and the mallet percussion instruments is rare and soon will disappear entirely. Even admission into the college and university bands and orchestras is being limited to students skilled in total percussion. Percussionists must be versatile in all areas of percussion to be of any value to the musical organization to which they belong. The only place these percussionists are going to receive a good start in their percussion training is in the school music program, our high school bands and orchestras. The time has come to give percussion students the same complete musical training given to other members of our school musical organizations.

Kenneth A. Mueller

Contents

TEACHING
TOTAL
PERCUSSION

1

How to Develop an Effective Total Percussion Program

Modern band music is becoming more demanding of the percussionist because composers are acknowledging and understanding the wide range of sounds and instruments available in the percussion section. They are writing for a greater number and variety of percussion instruments, and without ability in the total percussion, there will be occasions when your section will not be able to play the percussion parts.

Let's assume, for example, that you have a five member percussion section. Two players can play the snare drum and timpani, one plays only mallet percussion instruments, one plays only snare drum and the other has just started and can play only some of the accessory percussion instruments. This combination of abilities will limit the music that can be played. You could not, for instance, play any music which requires two mallet players. (This is becoming more common.) There are arrangements being published which require a complete drum set. This would not be possible with this section. Much of the percussion ensemble music would have to be eliminated because it requires two mallet players.

My research a few years ago showed that it was almost impossible to find a high school percussion student capable of playing all of the percussion instruments. In addition, I found that 25 per cent of the percussion students could not play the snare drum, 72 per cent did not know how to play the timpani and 94 per cent could not play the mallet percussion instruments. Hopefully, by now there has been some improvement in this but I feel there is still a long way to go. The snare drum, timpani and mallet percussion instruments should be the main areas of percussion instruction and should be incorporated into the lessons of every percussion student.

The difficulty of the percussion parts presents another problem with the section that has limited ability in the total percussion. If you have only one player who can play the mallet percussion instruments and one who can play the timpani, your choice of music will be dependent upon the ability of these students. True, they may be quite capable on their instruments but, on the other hand, they may not have the technical skill needed for some of the music. If every percussionist could play each of the percussion instruments, some would be better than others and the parts could be assigned according to their ability. Chances are there would be enough variety in their ability to play the parts from any arrangement the band would be able to play.

Percussion students not trained in the total percussion often do not think of the percussion as musical instruments. As a result, they lack a musical approach to performance. These students fail to understand the musicianship required to play the percussion correctly because they are specializing on only one percussion instrument. Their idea of a correct performance is often just playing the parts with the correct rhythm. By being trained in the total percussion, they learn to fit their part into the framework of the rest of the percussion and band parts. Percussion, like the other instruments, must be played with a conscious awareness of the other instruments and sounds around them.

Percussion students who are not trained in the total percussion are not properly prepared for continued music study at the college level. It is increasingly difficult for a percussion student to enter college as a music major playing percussion if he does not have a total percussion background. If admitted without this background, he will spend much of his four years of schooling catching up to the level of ability he should have reached before entering. Granted, this problem does not affect many of your students, but it will have a very adverse effect on the student who does want to continue his study of music.

The Challenge of Teaching Total Percussion

Once the director has seen the need for teaching total percussion he then has two major areas to develop for an effective total percussion program. He should know what the total percussion program includes and he must develop in his students a mature and positive attitude toward the total percussion.

What Does the Total Percussion Include?—Following is a list of the areas that should be included and developed when teaching the total percussion:

1) Instruction on all the percussion instruments. This is basic to the total percussion program. Instruction must continually take place in the three major areas of percussion study, i.e., snare drum, timpani and mallet percussion instruments. In addition, the percussion student should be taught how to play all the various accessory percussion instruments including bass drum, cymbals, woodblock, triangle, Latin American instruments and many more which you can find listed in Chapter 6. Note that I said the students must be *taught* how to play these instruments. There is a right and wrong way to play any of the percussion instruments. It generally takes just a short time to explain the correct way to play the accessory percussion instruments. Percussion students should also know how to play the drum set, as it can develop coordination skills. They should also have an intelligent approach to the marching percussion instruments.

2) A musical approach to the percussion. The percussion instruments must be taught as musical instruments, not rhythm instruments. The opposite approach has been used for too long. Involve the student in all phases of percussion. Train him to understand that there is more to the percussion than just playing a rhythm. The musical approach must be incorporated into every lesson and expected of the student in all rehearsals and performances.

3) A thorough application of the total percussion. Only through a complete program of involvement with the percussion instruments can the total percussion be taught effectively. This means the total percussion must be utilized in lessons, rehearsals, performances, solo and ensemble study, percussion ensemble and any other form of performance involving percussion.

4) Offer many varied experiences to each percussion student. This not only means that each student should have the opportunity to play all the percussion instruments, but he should also be given the chance to play in a band, orchestra, dance band (or some form of drum set experience) and percussion ensemble. He should also be given solo and ensemble experience. Much of this may already be a part of your present program, but these experiences should involve the total percussion.

Developing a Positive Attitude Toward the Total Percussion—If you are about to embark on a program of teaching the total percussion, it is likely you will have to start with high school students who have not had this type of instruction before. In initiating and maintaining a successful total percussion program you must have cooperative and interested students. It is best to explain to the students what the total percussion involves and why it should be taught. Tell the students of the benefits it will provide them and the band. Explain that learning to play only some of the percussion instruments is the same as other instrumentalists not knowing everything they need to know about their instrument. If they are not able to play *every* percussion part in a piece of band music, they are not adequately trained. Not all students will understand or accept this explanation, of course, because maturity and interest levels vary, but an explanation is still the best introduction to this type of program.

Once you have explained the concept of the total percussion to the students, get them involved in all the phases of percussion. In most cases, after the students begin to experience the many facets of total percussion they become increasingly more interested. Teach in a direct and intelligent manner. My experience has been that if the percussion is taught as a total unit, using the proper terms, teaching the correct techniques and emphasizing musicianship and versatility, the students will react favorably and can become more effective and cooperative in the band activities.

There may be some students who will not like playing the total percussion and decide to quit. My experience has been that the student you lose because of instituting a total percussion program is not really interested in putting much effort into learning to play. He started to play percussion not knowing what it really involved and was not interested enough to give that extra effort needed to play correctly. Chances are this same student has not contributed much to the band program up to this time and probably would not if he continued to play.

Once the total percussion program has been used in your school for a number of years there is little difficulty in developing in the students a good concept of what is involved. If the total percussion is taught from the very beginning, regardless of the age level, the students will not expect it to be taught any other way. If, on the other hand, you do not introduce the total percussion until the high school level you will need to continually work at developing cooperative attitudes and correct concepts of what percussion really involves. This is likely to lead to an increased percentage of percussion student drop-outs at the high school level. That is why I recommend that the total percussion be taught from the beginning, i.e., the time when your instrumental students begin playing.

The Relationship of the Percussion Instruments

In teaching the total percussion, emphasis cannot just be placed on the snare drum, for this is only a small part of the total percussion. There has been a trend to view the snare drum as the major percussion instrument with all the others as accessory instruments. In teaching total percussion you must place an equal emphasis upon the three major areas of the percussion: the snare drum, timpani and mallet percussion instruments. The study of these three instruments combined will include all the skills needed to play any of the percussion instruments. You will be using a total percussion approach by emphasizing the skills common to the various percussion instruments rather than the differences among them. When teaching any of the percussion instruments explain the similarities, then proceed to develop the special techniques required in each area.

There are many transfer skills in the areas of snare drum, timpani and the mallet percussion instruments, but the most important should be the grip. Although I recognize that there are many varying grips employed in the playing of percussion instruments, I advocate the use of the same matched grip on all percussion instruments. By using the same grip you will be developing the same muscle coordination regardless of the instrument. The wrist and arm action, which comprises the basic percussion stroke, will also be the same on each instrument. Because this book is based upon teaching total percussion in a unified manner, I refer only to the use of the matched grip on all percussion instruments. I am not suggesting, however, that you have your students change their rudimental snare drum grip if well developed, as this would certainly hamper their technical ability on the snare drum. It should be possible, however, for students to adjust their present grip for the timpani and/or mallet percussion to the method I advocate without affecting technical ability. In fact, students will find their technical skills improving once they have made the adjustment.

Reading skills, of course, will transfer from any percussion instrument and, in addition, the aural development gained on mallet percussion instruments can help in developing the aural skills needed to play and tune the timpani. The problem of sticking is similar on the timpani and mallet percussion instruments as is the choosing of the proper stick for the correct interpretation of a part.

There are also individual skills utilized in the major areas of percussion, and they too must be taught to develop the student's ability on each instrument. By emphasizing the similarities first, however, the student will feel he has a basic understanding of the instrument and can then work on the individual techniques. When teaching the total percussion the individual skills for each instrument are minimal. The snare drum, for instance, will require the additional study of the multiple bounce roll and the rudiments. Special timpani skills include ear training, mechanical tuning ability and reading the bass clef. Special skills for the mallet percussion instruments include reading in the treble clef, striking the bars and playing with from two to four mallets simultaneously.

There is also a relationship of skills found between the major areas of the percussion and the other percussion instruments. The marching percussion, for example, will utilize basic snare drum and timpani skills and possibly mallet percussion techniques. The drum set utilizes basic snare drum skills in addition to its own specialized skills which need to be developed. Most of the other accessory percussion instruments will utilize the same basic grip, stroke, wrist action and stance as used with the major percussion instruments. In addition, each accessory percussion instrument has its own specialized techniques which require special instruction for each student. Additional information about this can be found by referring to the appropriate chapters in this book.

2

How to Coordinate the Total Percussion Program with the Band Program

Scheduling Total Percussion Instruction

It is absolutely necessary that instruction of some sort be given to the percussion students if the total percussion is to be taught. It is impossible to teach the total percussion effectively if you meet your students only during the band rehearsal. If you are in a school situation where no time is provided for any type of instruction, your first job is to convince your administrators to allot instruction time during the school day for *each* band member. This must be done before you begin a program of total percussion instruction. Assuming that you see each student weekly, outside of band rehearsals, you probably can utilize the type of lessons you are already giving. However, because the scope and content of total percussion instruction is somewhat different from that of other instruments, there may be a more advantageous way to schedule for the percussion. Total percussion instruction generally needs more time than other instruments; however, the type and content of lesson used will best determine the length of time needed.

The private lesson, scheduled during the school day, is still the best type of lesson that can be given. It is usually scheduled during the student's free time, such as study hall or unscheduled class time. It can also be scheduled during the noon hour, before school or after school. Ideally, private percussion lessons should consist of either one 60-minute lesson or two 30-minute lessons per week. This, of course, is practically impossible to accomplish in the school situation except for a few instances in which the school might bring in a specialist to teach the various band instruments to the students. The amount of time that can be allotted to your students for private percussion instruction will depend upon your local situation.

There are two distinct advantages to private lessons for all students. First, scheduling is simplified, as it is much easier to find a time when one student is free to come to the music area for lessons than to find a time when a group of students are free. This type of lesson is also more flexible if you need to cancel or change a lesson time. The second and more important advantage is that of being able to work with each student individually, allowing him to progress at his own speed. This is especially important in percussion instruction as you will be teaching each student in many different areas at one time. It is probably safe to assume that each student will be at a different ability level in each area. Because of these advantages, I would even give priority to short private lessons instead of long group lessons.

If group instruction is necessary in your school because of the number of students or other scheduling problems, there are ways that it can be made more effective. Because you probably will not have many percussion students, and because at the high school level the percussion students are seldom free at the same time, a large group percussion lesson might not be possible. Instead, the group may have to be scheduled with only two or three students. If this is the case, try to schedule your group for a long lesson period. You can then spend part of the lesson with the entire group on general technical problems, ear training, theory and the accessory percussion instruments. Then divide the remaining time into short lessons with individual students concentrating on their particular instrument area. This will allow each student to work at his own speed while developing skills on the major percussion instruments and yet still being scheduled in a group lesson.

If time does not permit this type of lesson structure, try scheduling percussion students with similar ability into a group. This is difficult, however, as each student will be at a different ability level on each major percussion instrument.

One thing for certain is that the total percussion cannot be taught in heterogeneous groupings with other instrumental students. This becomes obvious when you consider teaching the drum set, timpani or snare drum and correlating this instruction with all the other band instruments. The instruction required in percussion is too specialized, and there are not enough similarities with the other band instruments to make this practical.

Lesson Content—Successful total percussion instruction is a result of carefully organized percussion lessons. As mentioned, percussion instruction must be based on the study of snare drum, timpani, and the mallet percussion instruments. In determining a lesson plan these three major areas of percussion study must be included along with time allotted for the study of theory, ear training, the drum set, marching percussion and the accessory percussion instruments.

There are five practical methods of organizing the total percussion instruction so that all necessary areas are covered:

1) Have the student work on all three major percussion instruments simultaneously. Spend part of each lesson on each instrument, theory, ear training and accessory percussion instruments. In addition, pick a few times during the year to devote to the drum set while giving up instruction on the stronger percussion instruments. A lesson organized in this way will require at least 60 minutes per week. This type of lesson can be divided as follows: 25 per cent for theory, ear training and accessory percussion instrument instruction, 25 per cent for

timpani, 25 per cent for mallet percussion instruments and 25 per cent for the study of the snare drum. These percentages can be altered to allow more time on the particular percussion instrument in which the student is weakest.

2) Have the student concentrate on his weakest instrument of the three major percussion instruments but continue with some study and exercises to maintain the other instrument skills. Periodically during the year time that is normally spent on the stronger instrument areas should be devoted to drum set instruction. This type of lesson might be divided as follows: 25 per cent for theory, ear training and accessory percussion instrument instruction, 50 per cent devoted to the weaker instrument area and 25 per cent toward brief exercises on the other two percussion instruments. In using this method, it is necessary to be aware of your student's ability in all three major areas of percussion so the emphasis can be switched when the student's ability changes.

A problem with this type of lesson is that a student could conceivably spend an entire year or more concentrating on only one phase of the percussion. This leads to an unbalanced program of percussion instruction which is contradictory to the total percussion approach. Also, care must be taken that the instruction and exercises provided in the stronger instrument areas remain challenging enough to require consistent practice.

3) Schedule two shorter lessons per week while teaching all three major percussion instruments simultaneously. With this type of lesson you should rotate instruction on the major percussion instruments listening to a different instrument each lesson. This type of lesson might be divided as follows: First lesson—25 per cent theory, ear training and accessory percussion instrument instruction and 75 per cent snare drum; Second lesson—25 per cent theory, ear training and accessory percussion instrument instruction and 75 per cent timpani; Third lesson—25 per cent theory, ear training and accessory percussion instrument instruction and 75 per cent mallet percussion instruments. Drum set instruction might be scheduled the same way with a fourth lesson added to include theory, ear training and accessory percussion instrument instruction

along with 75 per cent of the time spent on the drum set. Drum set instruction can also be provided by setting aside certain periods during the year to devote entirely to the drum set. This is often quite effective for some students, as it provides a break in the routine for the student.

A problem with this type of lesson is that the student might not practice on all the areas of percussion simultaneously but rather emphasize only that area which is part of the next lesson. Although this is not particularly desirable, the student is still being exposed to, and playing in, all the major areas of percussion.

4) Incorporate a schedule similar to the above on a weekly basis. With this type of lesson, instruction on the three major areas of percussion would be rotated each week and include some instruction on theory, ear training and the accessory percussion instruments in every lesson. This gives the student more time to prepare lessons on each instrument and utilizes less time when there is not much available for lessons. With most schools having about 36 weeks of school this would mean that the student would receive a maximum of 12 lessons on each major percussion instrument during the year. From this, time would have to be subtracted from drum set instruction. All solo, ensemble and marching percussion instruction can easily be incorporated into the regular lesson plan.

5) Have the student study each of the major percussion instruments separately. Divide the school year into sections and concentrate on one of the major percussion instruments during each section. Include within each lesson instruction in theory, ear training and the accessory percussion instruments. With this method the year can be divided into four sections as follows: eleven weeks of mallet percussion, eleven weeks of timpani, nine weeks of snare drum and five weeks of drum set instruction. The section can be adjusted to different lengths to allow more time in the student's weaker instrument area. Each lesson should be divided as follows: 20 per cent ear training and theory, 20 per cent accessory percussion instrument instruction and 60 per cent major percussion instrument instruction.

A problem with this type of lesson is that instruction is not provided on all the instruments year round. This method is quite useful when group or class lessons are scheduled.

Instruction on the marching percussion can be inserted into any of the lessons described above during the marching season. Usually the student needs only a brief explanation about the instrument he is to play, because they are all similar to the other percussion instruments. Additional instruction can then be incorporated into the band rehearsal time, as it will not be time consuming.

Practice Facilities—Percussion equipment is large, the number of instruments is often limited, and they are often all located in the same room. It is, therefore, necessary to provide special arrangements for percussion practice. A practice schedule should be set, providing each student with a time during his free time to practice the timpani, mallet percussion and accessory percussion instruments. A place should be provided to allow the student undisturbed practice. Arrangments should be made either to move the equipment out of the band room, keep other students from entering the room during practice times, or to acquire additional instruments which can be used for practicing purposes only.

Making the best use of the equipment you have will help in arranging practice facilities for your students. You can, for example, reduce the demand on certain percussion instruments by not concentrating on the same percussion instrument at the same time with each student. Also, the instruments you have can be utilized by more than one student. For example, there is usually only one set of timpani available. If this is a set of four timpani, it can be divided when students are practicing only two drum exercises or working on tuning exercises. Timpani sticking problems can be practiced on two field drums or tenor drums. This will permit two or more students to practice in the area of timpani at one time. Mallet percussion instruction need not be limited to just one instrument. It can be given on bells, xylophone, marimba or vibraphone. If these instruments are

available, you will be able to have four students practicing on
the mallet percussion instruments at one time.

If possible, the school should provide additional *practice*
instruments for student use. These should be kept in the
practice rooms and used for practicing instead of shifting and
dividing the equipment set up in the rehearsal room. The type
of instruments you will want for this are your older instruments, small 2½ or 3 octave marimbas and xylophones, and
some used timpani. Many of these instruments are available at
quite a reasonable cost.

Solo-Ensemble Experience—Most schools participate in some
form of solo-ensemble contest and therefore students are
probably receiving some form of solo and/or ensemble experience. The director should encourage students to perform this
type of music and this is best done by incorporating it into the
student's lesson. I suggest that students be encouraged to play
solos in their stronger instrument areas and ensembles in the
weaker areas. For example, if the student is a good timpanist,
he should play a timpani solo and some type of mallet
percussion and snare drum ensembles.

Percussion Ensemble—As described in Chapter 9, the percussion ensemble is essential toward good total percussion growth.
Every effort should be made to provide this experience for your
percussion students. The problem of scheduling is sometimes
complex as all percussion students should be involved. If you
have already organized brass or woodwind ensembles, clarinet
choirs, or even a percussion ensemble, you probably have an
idea when it is best to get this large a group together. The time
can vary considerably between schools because of respective
scheduling procedures. The rehearsals can often be scheduled
during an activity period, noon hour, after school or evenings. It
is best to have the rehearsal during the school day and you may
be fortunate enough to be able to do this. In my own
experience it was impossible to find any time during the school
day when the students were all free. I planned a one-hour
evening rehearsal approximately once a week, and varied the
nights we met, as some of the students had work schedules that

conflicted and could not be changed. In doing this I was able to have most of the students at each rehearsal but, if there was a student unable to attend on a particular night, he wasn't eliminated from the group because of being unable to make a rehearsal scheduled the same night every week.

As you can see, there are many possibilities of scheduling available in teaching the total percussion. Of these, some most certainly would fit into your particular situation. Perhaps you will be able to structure a different plan with the ideas presented here. The main thing is to be able to offer the student complete instruction in all the phases of the total percussion.

Budgeting for the Total Percussion

Lack of money is often thought the biggest argument against teaching the total percussion. Directors often feel that they are not well enough equipped with percussion instruments and will need to purchase a large number of the more expensive percussion instruments in order to get started. Naturally, this can present a problem in most schools and especially those where the budget is limited. This, however, is not usually the case.

It is probable that you already have much of the basic percussion equipment you need to start a total percussion program. Most schools have a snare drum, a set of two timpani and many of the accessory percussion instruments. If this is your situation the only additional instruments you will need to get started are a xylophone or marimba and a drum set. A 3½ octave xylophone can be purchased for under $400 and a basic drum set, which uses your present snare drum, suspended cymbals, etc., can be purchased for under $275. This is not an unreasonable expense to incorporate into the budget for one year. The purchase of a drum set can even be postponed, although it should be added as soon as possible to allow instruction to begin in this area.

You will then have the basic instruments needed to teach the three major percussion instruments and enough of the various accessory percussion instruments to get started in that area. Of course, there is much more equipment that will be needed, but these items will be enough to permit you to start teaching the total percussion. The rest of the accessory percussion instruments, additional major percussion instruments and practice instruments can be purchased on a gradual basis as the budget permits.

If you lack even the basic instruments, i.e., snare drum, timpani and some accessory percussion, your situation might necessitate a sizable purchase of percussion equipment. There are some ways in which you might be able to reduce the financial strain in this case. First, you might try obtaining an additional sum of money for your budget for a year only to get the program started. Talk to your administrator and explain the need for instituting a program of total percussion. Remember, once the initial purchases are made the rest of the equipment can be acquired gradually with the regular budget. Secondly, you might consider buying used instruments. This is not the best solution as it will prove difficult to find good used percussion instruments. It is worth looking into, however. Thirdly, music stores often will lease instruments to schools with the option of buying at a later date. This can reduce the initial amount of money you would need to get started.

After you have equipped your section adequately and can still budget money to add more percussion, buy additional practice instruments. For practice purposes I suggest getting small sized, student line or used equipment, and this need not be expensive equipment. Try to find adequate equipment at a minimum price.

Budget problems, therefore, are not a factor in starting a total percussion program unless you are very poorly equipped in the percussion instruments. With just a small initial outlay you can have the basic equipment needed to teach the total percussion. Once you have started, you can gradually add the rest of the percussion equipment needed. This can be done on a yearly basis and incorporated into the regular music budget.

3

How to Teach the Mallet Percussion Instruments Through Total Percussion

The mallet percussion instruments should be the basis of any percussion student's training. These instruments will help develop the percussionist's musical ability by creating an awareness of the melodic and harmonic properties of music otherwise left undiscovered in the study of the other percussion instruments.

I feel that training on the mallet percussion instruments will tend to develop all of the fundamental skills needed in percussion performance simultaneously and at concurrent levels of difficulty, while at the same time your students are beginning on perhaps the hardest and most complex of the percussion instruments. This is a much more efficient and sensible means of percussion instruction, especially when compared to the type of instruction presently given. For example, the typical percussion student starts his study of percussion with the snare drum where he learns the rudimental grip, coordination and advanced rhythmic understanding. That student then begins to study the timpani; his rhythmic knowledge is at an advanced level but his knowledge of interval relationships, his new matched grip and his reading of bass clef is at an elementary stage. Following proficiency on the timpani a student occasionally moves to the study of the mallet percussion instruments and he must again start over in terms of reading the treble clef, reading melodic lines and perhaps even learning another grip.

By basing the percussion student's training around the mallet percussion instruments you can develop a background of transfer skills which will make the teaching and performing of the other percussion instruments much easier. For example, the grip that is used when playing all of the mallet percussion instruments can be the same as that used on the timpani and snare drum. Students who use the marimba or xylophone as a basic training instrument, and these instruments are suggested for this purpose, need to develop a good single stroke roll. This same 'roll is essential in the playing of timpani and snare drum. A basic rhythmic understanding will be developed while studying the mallet percussion instruments that will transfer to the reading of all percussion music. The mallet percussion-trained student will develop a pitch relationship and sense for hearing intervals that can be of invaluable help when trying to tune the timpani. Also, the marimba student needs to read both the bass and treble clefs in his playing and the problem of learning how to read the bass clef when starting timpani is eliminated.

In view of this information I feel that the school music director should evaluate his percussion section seriously and consider the mallet percussion instruments as essential to the *training* of percussion students, as they are essential in the performing of today's band and percussion ensemble literature.

If the mallet percussion instruments are to be used as training instruments it is important that all percussion students be given the opportunity to perform on the instruments. Don't fall into the habit of placing your best percussion students on the mallet instruments and having them play all of the parts. This will certainly help insure good performance of the parts, but it is not good teaching of total percussion to your students.

The use of the mallet percussion instruments can offer many possibilities in their application to band arrangements. You need not be limited to using these instruments only when there is a special part written for them. The marimba and vibraphone, for example, have ranges which center in the general band tessitura and they blend well with both the brass and woodwind instruments. This makes them ideal instruments to use in strengthening weak solo lines, or weak harmonic accompaniments. They can also be used to accentuate a solo line or even substitute as the solo instrument. When using them for reinforcement of harmonic texture you can easily utilize two percussionists on a marimba.

While the bells and xylophone do not blend as well into the band sound, either can be used to punctuate and support solo lines in the high woodwinds and brass. The xylophone is particularly effective in complementing high staccato parts. By using marimba, vibraphone, xylophone and orchestra bells, you can make use of five of your percussion students strengthening weak harmonic and melodic sections of the band and adding new dimensions of tone color to the band sound. Not only does this help the band, but it helps your percussion students to become important musical performing members of your group and keeps them fully involved in the total percussion.

Description of the Mallet Percussion Instruments

Xylophone

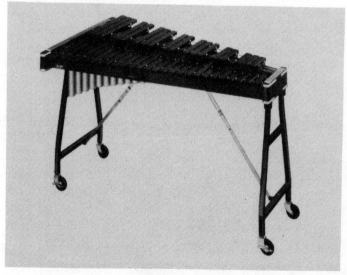

Photo courtesy of Ludwig Industries

Picture 3–1.

Tone: The characteristic tone of the xylophone can be described as brilliant and brittle. The xylophone is *usually* thought of in terms of being an orchestral instrument.

Range: The range of the xylophone is generally 3½ octaves, although instruments can be found in sizes ranging from 2½ to 4 octaves. Regardless, of the size of the xylophone, the top note remains the same; thus the larger the instrument the lower its range is extended. The written range of the xylophone is:

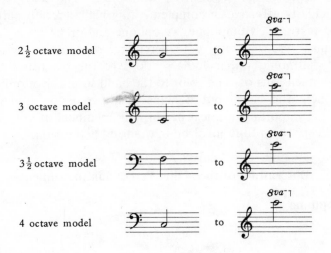

The xylophone is a transposing instrument and sounds one octave higher than written.

Physical Qualities: The xylophone has bars made of Honduras rosewood. These bars are thicker and shorter than those of the marimba. Under the bars are usually located resonator tubes which are closed pipes of steel or, more commonly, aluminum. The resonators are used to reinforce the sound of the mallet striking the wood bar. It is not necessary to have resonators on the xylophone, as the mallet striking the hard wood produces sufficient intensity to project the sound. However, without the resonator tubes the xylophone has a shorter and drier sound.

Mallets: Mallets of hard rubber, plastic or wood may be used on the xylophone for the best sound. Yarn-wound mallets do not have sufficient impact upon striking to produce a tone.

Brass mallets should never be used on the xylophone, as they will damage the keyboard.

Care: Proper care of the xylophone is important if you wish to maintain your instrument in good playing condition. Always keep the instrument covered with a clean cloth cover when not in use. Never set other instruments or objects on top of the keyboard as this can easily scratch the bars causing both unsightly appearance and discrepancies in tuning. Resonators are easily dented and care should be taken whenever moving the instrument that these are not damaged. Bars need to be cleaned and waxed periodically and cracked bars should be sent to the manufacturer for replacement. Guideposts are easily bent against the bars causing restriction of the vibrations of the bars. These should be checked periodically with bent posts being straightened and missing posts replaced. The insulators of the posts will dry out after a number of years and should be replaced. Suspension cords should be secure and tight.

In tuning the bars, the pitches are raised by shaving off the end of the bar, and lowered by shaving off the underside. As is evident, tuning the bars is a job for the professional. Most manufacturers will retune their own brand of instruments and occasionally will do other brands. I recommend that all mallet percussion instruments be sent to the manufacturer for tuning.

Marimba

Photo courtesy of J. C. Deagan, Inc.

Picture 3–2.

Tone: The characteristic tone of the marimba can be described as mellow, sonorous and warm. The marimba is *usually* thought of in terms of being a solo instrument.

Range: The range of the marimba varies from 2½ to 4 1/3 octaves. The 2½ and 3 octave marimbas are recommended only as starter instruments. The 3½ octave model will serve a useful purpose at the intermediate level, but for advanced, professional, or school use, the 4 or 4 1/3 octave model is recommended. The written range of the marimba is:

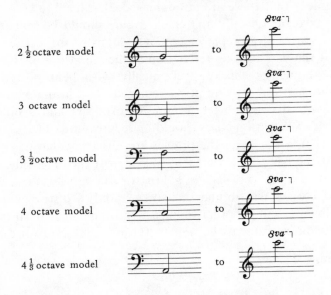

The written range of the marimba is essentially the same as the xylophone. Since the marimba is a non-transposing instrument and sounds at the written pitch, it actually plays one octave lower than the xylophone.

Physical Qualities: The marimba has bars made of Honduras rosewood. The bars are longer and thinner than those of the xylophone. The marimba must have resonator tubes to reinforce the sound. These are similar to the resonators on the xylophone except that they are twice as long since the marimba plays one octave lower.

Mallets: Generally, softer mallets are used on the marimba as this is more in keeping with the characteristic tone of the instrument. Mallets most frequently used are those made of soft, medium and medium-hard rubber, yarn-wound or felt. Occasionally hard rubber or wood mallets may be used. Never use very hard rubber or brass mallets as they will damage the keyboard.

Care: (See *Care:* under Xylophone, page 39.)

Orchestra Bells (Glockenspiel)

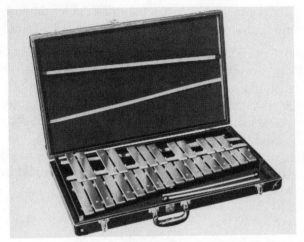

Photo courtesy of J. C. Deagan, Inc.

Picture 3—3.

Tone: The characteristic tone of the orchestra bells is a high-pitched, clear quality, bell-like tone.

Range: Practically all orchestra bells are made with a 2½ octave range. The written range for the orchestra bells is:

The orchestra bells are a transposing instrument sounding two octaves above the written pitch.

Physical Qualities: Quality-built orchestra bells have bars made of carbon-tempered steel. The resonating quality of this material, when struck by a hard mallet, is sufficient so that resonators are not required. Orchestra bells made with aluminum bars are inferior in tone to those having the steel bars.

Mallets: The following types of mallets may be used on the orchestra bells: (1) brass, (2) plastic, (3) hard rubber, (4) rawhide, and (5) wood. The choice of mallets, of course, will depend upon the preference of sound for the particular music. However, the brass mallet is perhaps the best all-around mallet to use on the bells. Never use the brass mallet on orchestra bells with aluminum bars, as they will damage the keyboard.

Care: Care is minimal for the orchestra bells. The instrument should be covered when not in use and other instruments and objects should not be placed on top. Check periodically to see that the guideposts are straight and not binding against the bars. Missing posts should be replaced. Be sure that the case cover is secure, especially in sets that have removable bars, and that handles and hinges are in good condition, as a set of steel orchestra bells is quite heavy. Orchestra bells should be tuned to an A=442.

Bell Lyre

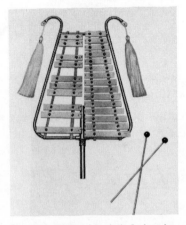

Photo courtesy of Ludwig Industries

Picture 3—4.

Tone: The tone of the bell lyre is similar to that of the orchestra bells although not as pure and refined. The tone quality is not as clear but projects well outdoors. This instrument should be used exclusively for marching purposes.

Range: The range of the bell lyre is always two octaves and is written as follows:

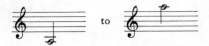

The bell lyre is a transposing instrument and sounds one octave higher than the written part.

Physical Qualities: Early bell lyres were made with steel bars. They contained ten to twelve interchangeable bars and the player carried the extra bars in a belt around the waist. This was later replaced by the chromatic bell lyre. Weight became a problem in carrying this instrument and the bars were later made of aluminum as they are today.

Mallets: Plastic or nylon mallets are most commonly used on the bell lyre, as they will produce the greatest projection of sound. Because of the technique of one-handed playing and the force of the stroke used, it is recommended that the mallets be a single unit of molded plastic or nylon and not have separate attached heads. The separate head mallets are more likely to break under the impact of playing. Both hard rubber and rawhide are also possible mallet choices but they will not produce the same intensity of tone as the nylon or plastic mallets. Never use brass mallets on the bell lyre, as the bars are made of aluminum and will be damaged.

Care: The bell lyre should be stored in a case or cover when not in use. Periodically check the guidepost screws which hold the bars in place to be sure that they are not bent, thus restricting the tone.

Vibraphone (Vibes)

Photo courtesy of Ludwig Industries
Picture 3–5.

Tone: The tone of the vibraphone is similar to the clear, bell-like quality of the orchestra bells except that it is lower pitched and much more mellow. A common characteristic of the tone is the vibrating quality which can be produced mechanically by the instrument.

Range: Vibraphones are produced in either 2½ or 3 octave sizes with the 3 octave size being the more popular and recommended size. The written range of the vibraphone is as follows:

The vibraphone is a non-transposing instrument which sounds at the written pitch.

Physical Qualities: The bars of the vibraphone are constructed of an aluminum alloy. Resonator tubes are required and are similar to those on the marimba with the exception of the pulsators located at the top of each resonator under the bar. These pulsators are small fan-like discs which are connected together and turned by means of an electric motor. When in operation these pulsators give the vibraphone its characteristic vibrating sound and prolong the sustained tone. Some vibraphones have a variable speed control on the motor to control the speed of the vibrations.

In addition, the vibraphone contains a damper pedal which is used to regulate the length of resonance. This pedal operates in a manner which is similar to the sostenuto pedal on the piano. Tones can be sustained only by pressing the damper pedal down. This pulls a felt covered bar away from the underside of the bars, thus allowing them to ring freely; releasing the pedal stops the tone. The damper bar is necessary because the length of resonance on the vibraphone is much longer than on the xylophone, marimba or orchestra bells.

Mallets: Soft, medium and medium-hard rubber, yarn-wound and felt mallets are the most commonly used on the vibraphone. Hard rubber, wood and plastic may be used for special effects but are not consistent enough with the tone quality of the instrument to warrant general use. Never use brass mallets on the vibraphone, as the bars are made of aluminum and will be damaged.

Care: Bars should be cleaned and polished periodically. The instrument should be covered when not in use and other instruments or objects should not be placed upon it. Guidposts need to be checked, with bent and missing posts corrected. Suspension cords should be tight and replaced when wear begins to show. The damper pedal will need occasional adjustment to be sure that it is operating correctly with a minimum of foot action. The electric motor should be properly maintained and belts and pulleys should be kept in good condition. Check belts periodically to be sure that they are not slipping. Vibraphones, as all the mallet percussion, need to be retuned occasionally. This should be done by the manufacturer.

Chimes

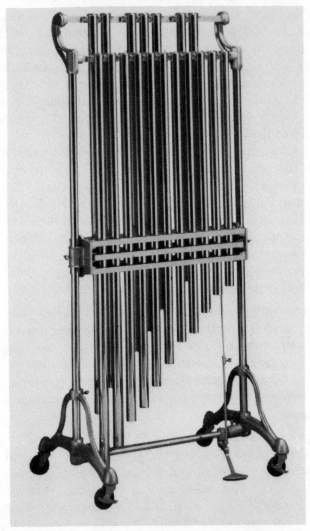

Photo courtesy of J. C. Deagan, Inc.

Picture 3–6.

Tone: Originally, the main purpose of chimes was to imitate the sound of church bells. Its tone is very similar to this sound.

Range: The range of the chimes is usually 1½ octaves. The written range of the chimes is:

Chimes are a non-transposing instrument and sound at the written pitch.

Physical Qualities: Chimes consist of a rack upon which are suspended tubes made of a relatively hard brass-steel alloy. The tubes are made in either 1, 1¼ or 1½ inch diameters. As the tonal strength of the chime is directly related to the amount of metal in the tube, the larger the diameter, the greater the tonal depth and carrying power. Most chimes made today are equipped with a damper pedal similar to the one found on the vibraphone. The action of the pedal differs with different manufacturers, some damp when the pedal is down and others when the pedal is up.

Mallets: Chime mallets are usually made from tightly rolled rawhide with a wooden handle. A wooden mallet can also be used or, for a more subdued tone, a wooden mallet with leather covered ends. The chime mallet's shape is somewhat different from the mallets used on the rest of the mallet percussion instruments and looks like a hammer. Do not use metal mallets on the chimes unless they are specifically requested in the part, as they tend to damage the tubes and are not consistent with the best tone quality of the instrument.

Care: The chimes should be covered when not in use. The single most important part of the chimes which should be checked regularly is the suspension cords. They should be replaced at the first sign of wear or you may find your chimes falling off the rack in the middle of a concert. The damper pedal should be checked periodically to be sure it is operating with the minimum of foot action. Be sure that the rack is strong and secure at all times, but especially after moving the instrument, as it must support a considerable amount of weight.

Playing Technique

Xylophone, Marimba, Vibraphone and Orchestra Bells

The playing techniques required for these instruments are essentially the same; therefore I have grouped them together as a matter of convenience. Any significant differences in playing techniques will be noted as they occur.

The Grip: Two Mallet Playing—The shaft of the mallet if held primarily between the thumb and index finger. This forms a pivoting point for the mallets. The following steps will help you obtain the correct grip:

1. Open hand up with palm facing you.

2. Lay the mallet diagonally across the fingers with the end of the mallet starting at the base of the little finger and extending upward to cross the first joint of the index finger (Picture 3-7).

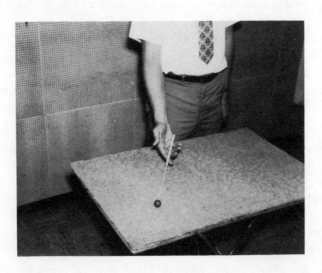

Picture 3—7.

3. Place the thumb on the shaft at the point where it crosses the index finger. Thumb should point toward the head of the mallet (Picture 3-8).

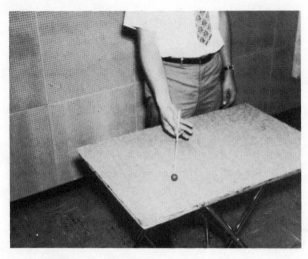

Picture 3—8.

4. Close fingers loosely around shaft (Picture 3-9).

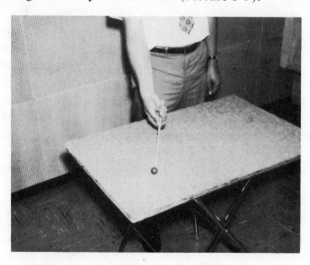

Picture 3—9.

5. Turn the hand so that the palm is facing down. Stick is now in the correct position with the pivotal point between the thumb and index finger (Picture 3-10).

Picture 3—10.

6. The grip is the same for the other hand.

For the xylophone, marimba and vibraphone the mallets should be held near the end of the shafts. Because the orchestra bells are a smaller instrument, the sticks are held somewhat closer to the head of the mallet. Once the grip is correct, arms should be slightly away from the side of the body with the hands in front of the body for freedom of movement. Mallets should meet at about a 90 degree angle on the bars and should extend upward from the plane of the keyboard at about a 10 degree angle.

Four mallet playing—There are two grips commonly employed in four mallet playing.

Method One

1. Lay the mallets on the keyboard with the shaft of the outside mallet crossing over the top of the shaft of the inside mallet, thus forming an X.

2. Place the second finger underneath both sticks at the place that they cross so that the inside mallet rests at the first joint of that finger (Picture 3-11).

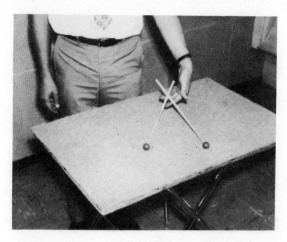

Picture 3–11.

3. Place the index finger above the center of the formed X and the thumb to the inside of the X (Picture 3-12).

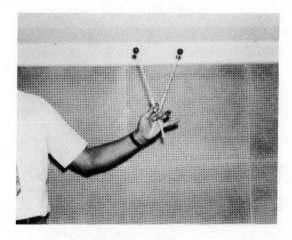

Picture 3–12.

4. The third finger reaches over to wrap around the end of the outside mallet and the fourth finger wraps around the end of the inside mallet (Picture 3-13).

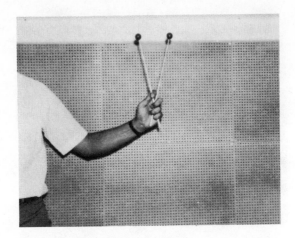

Picture 3—13.

5. Sticks should be held with the palm of the hand facing down (Picture 3-14).

Picture 3—14.

6. The space between the mallets is increased by the use of the thumb and index finger. The index finger is curled from an outstretched position to a grasping position around the inside mallet shaft while at the same time the thumb slides upward along the shaft, goes over the top and turns inward (Picture 3-15).

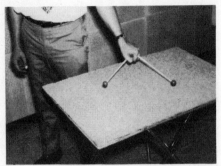

Picture 3—15.

7. The grip is the same for the other hand.

When striking the bars with this method, both sticks should strike simultaneously.

Method Two (The Musser Grip)

1. There is no crossing of the mallets in this method.

2. The outside mallet is grasped with the third and fourth fingers and extended out from between the second and third fingers (Picture 3-16).

Picture 3—16.

3. The inside mallet is held between the thumb and index finger with the second finger wrapping loosely around the stick (Picture 3-17). (This is similar to the conventional single stick grip.)

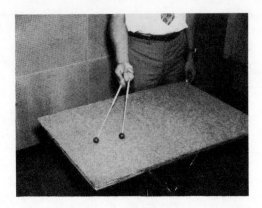

Picture 3–17.

4. Palms should face downwards when playing with this grip (Picture 3-18).

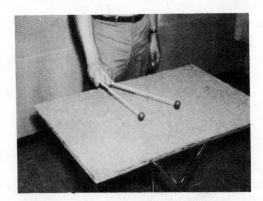

Picture 3–18.

5. The space between the mallets is increased by regulating the thumb and index finger.

When using this method the sticks may strike either simultaneously or in a staggered fashion depending on the effect desired. The staggered fashion roll is usually more effective on the marimba in solo use.

Three mallet playing—The three mallet grip is a combination of the single mallet grip in one hand (usually the right) and either of the double mallet grips in the other hand.

The Stroke: Hold the mallet about two or three inches above the bar. Strike with a quick flick of the wrist and lift the mallet away from the bar as though drawing the tone from the bar. Return the mallet to the same position above the next note to be struck. For faster playing you should maintain the same concept but reduce the amount of lift to insure accuracy.

The mallets should move in a straight "up and down" motion which is perpendicular to the bars. This will be fairly easy to control providing the player takes care to keep the palms of his hands facing down and the hands parallel to the floor. Avoid both a rolling motion and a sideways stroke when striking the bars, as both tend to make the stroke less accurate.

The stroke concept is the same for two, three and four mallet playing.

The bars should be struck in the center, directly above the resonators for maximum tone resonance. The same would also apply for the orchestra bells and xylophone without resonators. For greater speed and accuracy in rapid playing, the bars of the upper keyboard may be struck at the ends closest the player with little sacrifice in tone quality. Care should be taken, however, to avoid striking the area where the suspension cord passes through the bar as this is a nodal point, thus lacking resonance. In three and four mallet playing, when one hand is playing on bars in both the upper and lower keyboard, the mallets should strike the end of the upper keyboard and the center of the lower keyboard note.

The Stance: The player should stand close enough to reach the center of the bars in the upper keyboard without excessive reaching. This will usually be about six to ten inches away from the instrument. The feet should be comfortably spaced and the body centered within the range of the music to be performed. Avoid "walking" or crossing the feet while playing, as this will tend to throw the performer off balance thus reducing the accuracy and uniformity of his playing. If the range of the part is large, the performer will need to move somewhat. This should be done with either a sliding or shuffling motion of the feet.

The Performance: To help in the reading of music at the beginning stages, the music stand should be placed in the center of the instrument and kept as low as possible. This will help keep the student from losing his place as he looks from the music to the keyboard. Ultimately, the student should strive to develop peripheral vision, much like that of the pianist, which will eliminate this need.

Rolls—The single stroke roll is used on all mallet percussion instruments. For xylophone and orchestra bells, the speed of the roll should be constant. Because of the greater resonance in the lower register of the marimba and vibraphone a fast roll on these notes will tend to cancel out the sound. Therefore, you should roll more slowly on the low register notes and faster on the high register notes. Rolls are utilized regularly on the xylophone and marimba and only rarely on the orchestra bells and vibraphone.

It is a good idea to start the study of the single stroke roll at an early age in order for a student to have a competent roll when he reaches high school. If the mallet percussion instruments are not available at the elementary or junior high level, careful study of this roll on the snare drum (using the matched grip) and timpani will also prepare the student for rolling on the mallet percussion instruments.

Students should learn to start their rolls with either hand. In legato playing (i.e., a continuous roll while changing notes to follow the music) the mallet nearest the next note should lead in the change, thus either hand will have to lead. When changing notes the bars should be approached and left smoothly with a minimum of time and motion. Care should be taken that there is no space between the rolled notes and that no false accents occur when moving.

Sticking—Alternate sticking (L.R.L.R.) is the primary method used when playing. Double sticking (L.L. or R.R.) should be used only to avoid excessive cross sticking. Deviations from the alternate sticking pattern should be marked in the music so that the piece is practiced the same way each time. In so doing, the sticking, regardless of how complex, will become automatic after a period of practice. The choice of sticking can best be solved by choosing the way in which the least time and motion are involved, while maintaining a steady beat and consistent volume, and avoiding excessive cross sticking and false accents. Remember that the resultant sound is of primary importance, even over the choice of sticking, but that the choice of sticking will affect that resultant sound.

To maintain a uniform sound while playing, the following points should be kept in mind:

1. Raise the mallets to an equal height while playing;
2. Keep the grip and hand position identical in both hands;
3. Maintain equal force of the stroke from each hand;
4. Play in the center of each bar or at the end of the bars of the upper keyboard when necessary. Avoid playing on the node;
5. Use only the wrist and fingers in making the stroke and no arm motion from the elbow except for moving the mallets horizontally across the keyboard;
6. Take care to avoid false accents which often occur when moving quickly from note to note;
7. Execute rolls somewhat softer when playing with single notes and rolls intermixed, as rolls tend to project more than single notes.

Pedal Technique for Vibraphone: The tone of the vibraphone is usually sustained by the use of the pedal instead of a single stroke roll. When it is pressed down the tone will ring freely; release the pedal and the tone stops. This pedal technique is employed whether the pulsators are in use or not.

Another means of stopping the tones from ringing on the vibraphone is by the use of the mallets or fingertips. The note which is sounding is stopped by touching it with either the mallet or the fingertip at the same time that the next note is struck. The advantage of this method is that it will produce a sustained line with no overlapping of tones and will eliminate the break in the sound due to the damper pedal action. A much more legato style of playing is available with this technique.

When playing the vibraphone without using the pulsators, care should be taken that they be in a vertical position thus leaving the resonators open. If the pulsators are left in a horizontal position, you are in effect removing the resonators from the instrument and the resultant sound will not have a very good quality.

The Choice of Mallets: (Also see *Mallets,* under the description of each instrument.) The choice of mallets is a personal decision that the performer and director must make. The weight, size and material of the mallet must be chosen to be appropriate with the music to be performed and the register in which it is written.

For example, if a piece is written for the marimba which is to be soft and primarily in the low register, soft yarn mallets might be a wise choice. On the other hand if the piece is to be played loudly and in the middle and upper registers, a hard rubber mallet might be a better choice. A loud passage in the low register might use a soft rubber mallet. If you have a xylophone part which should blend into the ensemble sound, a medium-hard rubber mallet might work well. If this same part is supposed to project through the ensemble, you would probably want to use a plastic mallet.

The most important thing to remember is that most parts will call for a variety of sounds and will lie in different ranges of the instrument. As the mood, style or range of the piece changes, so must the choice of mallets. It is a good idea to mark the mallet changes as needed in the music so that the changing is remembered and practiced along with the piece. Do not have all your xylophone parts played with a plastic mallet, all your marimba parts with a soft rubber mallet, all of your orchestra bell parts with a brass mallet and all of the vibraphone parts with yarn-wound mallets. Use your imagination and experiment to match the mood, style and requirements of the piece with appropriate mallets.

When using mallets with rattan shafts, be sure that they are of uniform thickness and flexibility and avoid those which have any major warping. The use of mallets with synthetic shafts will avoid these problems. For this reason I would suggest the fiberglass shafts for school use.

Bell Lyre

The Grip: It is generally recommended that the bell lyre be played with the right hand only (left hand for left-handed players). The grip of the mallet is the same as for the other mallet percussion instruments except that the palm of the hand should face the instrument rather than the floor. (See Playing Technique for Xylophone, Marimba, Vibraphone and Orchestra Bells.)

The Stroke: The stroke used for the bell lyre is the same as on the other mallet percussion instruments. Be sure always to strike in the center of each bar.

Carrying the Bell Lyre: The bell lyre is carried in a carrying holster which is worn over the right shoulder and under the left arm (just the reverse for left-handed players).

The instrument should be carried at such a height that the low "F" bar is level with the player's eyes. This height will provide the opportunity for striking all the bars at an equal angle. If the instrument is carried lower than this, difficulty will occur in trying to play the lower notes. The bell lyre has a telescopic staff which adjusts to accommodate players of various heights. The left hand should grasp the staff immediately below the lyre and hold it slightly to the left of the player. This will provide a good angle at which to strike the bars while at the same time providing good vision straight ahead of the player.

The Performance: The use of only one mallet is recommended when playing the bell lyre. When using two mallets and a special carrying holster, you will find the instrument still tends to sway back and forth and up and down while marching, often causing playing errors. By playing with only one hand, you enable the other hand to stabilize the instrument while marching. Also, the use of one hand will provide a greater space between notes, thus eliminating some of the overlapping of sound from the freely ringing bars.

Most bell lyre parts will need to be arranged by the director, as the parts that are published are usually too difficult to perform with one hand, or are so complex that they will result in much overlapping of sounds. Write the bell lyre part to accentuate the main notes of the melodic line. The part should consist mainly of quarter notes and half notes. This type of part will be much more effective for use on the march.

The Bell Lyre in Concert Use: The bell lyre is a marching instrument and should *not* be used in concert performance. The three main reasons for this are: _____

1. The quality of the sound will not equal that of the steel bars of the orchestra bells;
2. The instrument transposes only one octave up instead of two as do the orchestra bells and, therefore, will sound one octave lower than the orchestra bells;
3. The bell lyre has a different range from the orchestra bells and many times the bell part needs to jump into different octaves in order to be played on a bell lyre.

Chimes

The Grip: Although the chime mallet is quite different in shape from any of the other mallet percussion mallets, the grip is still essentially the same. The mallet is held firmly in the hand with the thumb and index finger opposite each other. The grip will resemble somewhat the way one would hold a hammer.

The Stroke: The stroke is the same as for any of the other mallet percussion instruments. Each chime tube has a cap at the top. The tube should be struck at a 45 degree angle on the rim of this cap. Never strike the tube on the side, as this will dent the tube and affect its intonation, and do not strike with a downward stroke on the top of the tube, for this will tend to weaken the suspension cords. Either way will also produce an inferior tone from the instrument.

When playing on the front rack of the chimes, the mallet should be held halfway between a vertical and horizontal position. When playing on the back of the rack the mallets must be held horizontally in order to avoid accidentally hitting the front row of tubes.

The Performance: Old-fashioned chimes did not have a damper pedal and therefore one hand was needed for damping the chimes. It is from this that the concept of playing the chimes with only one hand evolved. With the advent of the modern chime and the damper pedal, the hand damping technique is no longer required. Chimes should, therefore, be played with two hands. Not only will this technique be necessary for many of the more difficult chime parts, but it will also make the playing of all chime parts much easier.

4

How to Teach the Timpani Through Total Percussion

The Timpani and Its Relationship to the Total Percussion

It is important to remember when training students in the total percussion that each instrument will require special techniques. Although there are some skills which can and should transfer from the other percussion instruments to the timpani, you would be taking the wrong approach if you instructed your students to play the timpani in the same manner as the snare drum or the mallet percussion instruments. Even though the grip of the sticks is the same (assuming the use of the matched snare drum grip) and the stroke is basically the same, the instruments are different and the students must be taught many specific techniques which apply only to the timpani.

One of the most important techniques required on the timpani is that of tuning. This is perhaps the area where school timpanists have the most trouble and the least training. The timpani must be struck in the proper place with the proper stroke on a head that is correctly balanced in order to sound at the correct pitch with a proper tone. To do this requires careful instruction in playing techniques, repeated sessions in tuning and the aural development of the student.

The study of the timpani provides an integral part of the student's training in the total percussion; that is, the development of an awareness of pitch and interval relationships. If a student begins his percussion study on just the snare drum, pitch and interval relationships are not needed and we often find students reluctant to do much in the way of aural development. Later, if and when he begins to play the timpani, he is more likely to approach it as being a new challenge in sticking and hand coordination without any regard to intonation.

This points up the value and necessity of teaching the total percussion and working simultaneously in the three areas of snare drum, timpani and the mallet percussion. The study of the mallet percussion at the beginning of the student's training should develop a feeling for, and understanding of, intervals. In fact the singing of intervals and matching of pitches can easily be incorporated into this period of study. By studying the timpani at the same time, you can apply this knowledge to the exercises in tuning. It is also necessary at this time to introduce some basic theory of intervals, keys and harmonic structure.

The main objectives to be developed during the student's study of the timpani would be an aural understanding, the actual tuning of the timpani, understanding of the proper stroke, the striking areas on each timpano and a physical coordination for hands and arms while playing on two or more timpani.

Physical Characteristics of the Timpani

Photo courtesy of Ludwig Industries

Picture 4–1.

Size and Range: Timpani are commonly available in eight different sizes. The practical range of each timpano is about a 5th and this corresponds to the bowl size. The range of the eight common timpani is as follows:

23 inch bowl	
24 inch bowl	
25 inch bowl	
26 inch bowl	
28 inch bowl	
29 inch bowl	
30 inch bowl	
32 inch bowl	

Timpani with plastic heads generally are capable of extending their range one step higher than those listed above.

It is customary to have the basic pair of timpani consisting of either the 25" and 28" sizes or the 26" and 29" sizes. In either case the range of the basic pair of timpani should comprise a full octave with the low timpano extending from low "F" to "C" and the high timpano from "Bb" to "F". Most schools will already have one pair or the other. If you are going to buy new timpani, however, I would recommend the 25'' and 28'' sizes, as their desirable range coincides with the tonal range needed for the basic pair of timpani. This results in a slightly better tone.

The purpose of adding more timpani to the basic pair is to extend their range, to give a greater flexibility in the choice of timpani for the required pitches, and to reduce the number of tuning changes within a piece. When adding a third timpano to the basic pair I have found more use for a larger size. Either the 30'' or 32'' size timpano would be satisfactory but, if you can budget for it, the 32'' size would be the best. You will want to extend the range as low as possible. If you do not have a regular need for the low "C" which is available on the 32'' timpano, you can tune it to the range of the 30'' timpano thus making it more functional for most playing. This will, however, depreciate the tone quality somewhat. When adding a fourth timpano it should be either the 23'' or 24'' size. The 23'' drum will give you better tone quality in the higher range. Because the range of the timpani part will often go above an "F" I would suggest this size as the best choice.

A set of four timpani is becoming essential to play much of the music encountered at the high school level. Also, four timpani can be put to good use in all timpani parts to help you avoid awkward tuning changes while playing. While this gives your students more experience with playing on three or four timpani, don't overlook the importance of developing skills in rapid and accurate tuning.

The Bowl: Timpani bowls are usually made of copper or fiberglass. Historically, copper has been used but modern engineering has developed the fiberglass bowl to a fairly acceptable level. The main detriment to the fiberglass bowl is that it cannot produce the quality of tone available from the copper bowl. I recommend the use of the fiberglass bowl at the elementary and junior high level because they are less expensive, lighter in weight, and they resist denting or other damage which might occur due to more careless handling by younger children. At the high school level I recommend only the copper bowl timpani. Older students should have a better understanding of the care and proper handling of the instrument and should also be able to contend with the extra weight. The superior tone given by the copper bowl and the necessity for this quality of tone at the high school level can easily justify the expense.

The Tuning Mechanisms: There are many styles of tuning mechanisms used on timpani. Pedal timpani are superior to hand-tuned timpani, as they allow the player to make faster tuning changes. Any timpano which has all of its tuning mechanism and tuning rods outside of the bowl is going to produce a better tone. I have listed below a few of the more popular types, with the first three being the most practical for high school use:

1. The Spring Tension Pedal—In this style a pedal is used to adjust the head tension. Pushing down on the toe of the pedal will increase the tension and returning the heel will decrease the tension. A spring located within the pedal mechanism counteracts the head tension thus allowing the pedal to remain fixed at any position in which it is set. The Ludwig Standard Symphony Model timpani is an example of this style.
2. The Friction Clutch Pedal—In this style the pedal slides up and down along a fixed post. As the pedal is pushed down the tension of the head increases. When the player removes his foot from the pedal, a clutch mechanism engages the post and prevents the pedal from returning to the position of least tension. Pressing the front of the pedal forward with the toe releases the clutch mechanism. All Slingerland model timpani use this type of mechanism.
3. The Ratchet Pedal—In this style pedal a ratchet is attached to the pedal. A trigger device which is activated with a sideways motion of the foot allows you to move the pedal into any position along the ratchet. Releasing the trigger holds the pedal in that spot. The Ludwig Dresden model timpani utilizes this style pedal.
4. The Hand Crank—In this style the crank is connected to the tuning rods. As the crank is turned in a clockwise direction the tuning rods are pulled downward, thus

increasing the head tension. The Ludwig Concert Machine timpani have the hand crank mechanism.

5. The Rotary Bowl—In this style, tuning rods are attached inside the bowl in such a way that as the bowl is rotated, they draw down on the counterhoop and increase the tension.

6. The Chain Style Mechanism—In this style all the tuning lugs are connected together by means of a chain. As you turn any one of the lugs, all of the others will turn an equal amount.

The Timpani Heads: Timpani heads are made of calfskin or plastic. Historically the calfskin head was the only type used and it is still capable of producing the best quality tone today. The plastic head, however, has been improved since it was first introduced and the resultant tone is no longer unsatisfactory. Calfskin heads must be checked for balance and intonation each day before playing in order to achieve superior tone, and chances are that in the school situation this will not be done. The advantage of the plastic head is that it is not affected by humidity. This makes for easier and more consistent tuning, fewer maintenance problems and generally longer life than the calfskin head. For these reasons I recommend plastic timpani heads for school use.

The Maintenance of the Timpani

When not in use the timpani should be covered with either a cardboard or masonite cover to protect the heads and a full drop cloth cover to protect the body of the instrument. Heads should be kept clean, as it will help preserve the life of your sticks and maintain good tone quality. Both plastic and calfskin heads should be wiped off weekly with a clean damp cloth. Do not leave any water standing on the head when doing this. Tuning lugs should be lubricated lightly with Vaseline. Dents in the bowl can be removed by pounding carefully from the inside of the bowl with a hard rubber hammer.

Adjusting the Collar: (Calfskin heads only) Listed below are some terms which the music instructor needs to be familiar with when reading this section:

Flesh hoop—a metal hoop to which the head is attached.

Counter-hoop—the outer hoop to which the lugs are attached. The counter-hoop rests on top of the flesh hoop and head, and is used to pull the head down, thus raising the pitch.

Collar—the distance from the rim of the bowl to the top of the counter-hoop. A collar ranging from 1/2" to 3/4" will give you optimum tonal response.

The procedure for setting the collar is the same on a new calfskin head as for re-setting the collar on an old head. The head is placed on the timpani with the counter-hoop in place. Soak down the *top* of the head with a clean cloth and room-temperature water being careful not to get any water between the flesh hoop and the counter-hoop. As the head becomes soaked it will soften and become pliable. When it is evenly soaked, set the pedal or crank in the highest note position, then adjust the lugs to form a 5/8" collar around the entire circumference of the head. The head must then dry slowly in a draft-free location. This process can be achieved by placing a large piece of cardboard or masonite across the LUGS. (Do not touch the head.) This will slow the drying process and will keep drafts off the head. After dry, (about 24 hours), it will be necessary to retune the head.

To help maintain your collar once it is set, do the following:

1. In dry weather keep tension on the head when not in use or it will shrink and the collar will become too small.

2. In damp weather release the tension from the head after use, especially if it was necessary to turn the lugs down in order to get the head into tune before starting. If this is not done the collar will become too big.

As humidity does not affect plastic heads, the collar should remain as set at the factory.

Balancing the Head: Strike the timpano head in the playing area adjacent to each tuning lug. It is most likely that you will notice different pitches coming from different sections of the head. A balanced head will produce the exact same pitch regardless of where you strike on the head. A balanced head is essential as it will produce a richer and more sonorous tone and provide accurate intonation at all times on the timpani. Also, on the spring-tension style pedal, an unbalanced head will cause this pedal to operate improperly.

If the timpano is not in tune or the head not balanced, proceed as follows. Set the pedal or tuning handle to the low note position. (If, on the spring tension model the pedal will not stay at this position, hold it in place with your foot.) Adjust the tuning lugs so that the head sounds at the correct lowest pitch for that particular timpano. Then adjust the pedal or tuning handle to raise the pitch about a fourth. (This need not be accurate, it is just easier to hear the pitch differences at a higher pitch.) Choose one tuning lug as a "master" pitch and tune all the other lugs so that the tone adjacent to them will sound the same as the one adjacent to the "master" lug. As opposite tuning lugs affect each other the pattern shown in the illustration below will work best in tuning. Remember to retune to the "master" lug between each tuning.

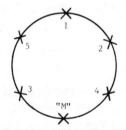 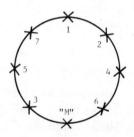

Using the tip of one finger strike the head firmly so that the true fundamental pitch will sound. The sound which continues to resonate contains too many overtones to be used for tuning purposes. By placing a small soft cloth or mute in the center of the head, you will eliminate most of these overtones from sounding. Be sure to damp the head completely each time before striking at the next lug. It will take some practice to learn to recognize whether a pitch is sharp or flat to the "master" pitch. However, a little experimenting with listening and adjusting the head will soon overcome the problem.

Once all tuning lugs have been adjusted, check around the circumference for uniform pitch and adjust where needed in the same manner. When the head is balanced, return the pedal or tuning handle to the lowest pitch and check to be certain that the pitch is correct. If it is not, adjust each lug an *equal amount* to correct the pitch and check the balance again.

On the spring tension pedal you may need to adjust the tension control once the head is balanced in order to make the pedal work properly. If the pedal moves *down* when released there is not enough tension in the spring. Tighten this by turning the tension control in a clockwise direction. If the pedal rises when released, there is too much tension in the spring and you should turn the spring control in a counter-clockwise direction.

Because the resistance and stresses on the timpani head change with playing, and because tuning lugs may be altered between playings, the timpani heads should be checked for balance before each rehearsal. This procedure can be done very quickly if it is done regularly. Because it needs to be done regularly, the technique of balancing the heads should be taught to your students.

Removing Extraneous Noises: If you notice a rattling sound when playing, check for the following:

1. Loose screws, rods or other fittings on the timpani
2. Loose material inside the timpani bowl
3. Music stand touching the timpani and responding to its vibrations
4. Sympathetic vibrations setting other equipment or percussion instruments into vibration.

Locate the cause of the rattle, then tighten, remove or pad the offending area.

If the timpano "squeaks" when tuning, lubrication is needed where the head makes contact with the rim of the bowl.

Remove the head, clean the rim and inside the head, and lubricate the bowl edge with paraffin. (Vaseline may be used for plastic heads.) Be sure to retune the heads when you replace them.

If there is a "buzzing" sound from the head when playing certain notes the following will most likely be the cause:

1. Dirt between the counter-hoop and flesh hoop
2. Dirt between the head and the rim of the bowl
3. Unequal tension of the head.

When this happens, remove the head, clean the bowl rim, clean inside and outside the head and counter-hoop, lubricate lightly as above, replace head and balance carefully.

Playing Techniques for the Timpani

The Arrangement of the Timpani: It is customary to arrange the timpani so that the larger drum is to the left. Place the timpani in a semi-circle so that they are all an equal distance from the performer. This is especially important when using three or four timpani. When tuning the timpani to the required pitches of any particular piece have the lower pitches to the left. Keeping this uniform makes it much easier to remember the location of the various pitches while playing.

The European system of arranging the timpani is just the opposite, but there is no particular advantage to either system.

The Body Position: When using two timpani stand so the body faces the music stand which is always located between these two timpani. When using three timpani, face the middle one, and with four timpani face the music stand but stand farther back. The body should be situated so that no timpani are behind the player. Move only the arms when playing from one timpano to the other. Do not rotate the upper torso. The feet should be comfortably spaced with the right foot slightly ahead of the left. The timpano on the left is the larger and you must therefore play farther toward the center of the head in order to reach the proper playing area. By having your right foot forward you will tend to lean to the left and the placement of the stick in the proper playing area will be simplified. When using three or four timpani the player will need to move his feet more often to establish a good position. This should be done with a shuffling action.

In most cases it is better for the timpanist to stand while playing. The exception would be when the piece calls for complex tuning changes. A stool would then be advisable to enable both feet to be placed on the pedals for tuning changes.

The Grip: The grip which I recommend for the timpani is exactly the same as used on the mallet percussion instruments (see page 48, Chapter 3). By using a uniform grip you are training the muscles of the hand to react the same, regardless of the percussion instrument; thus you will tend to develop better hand control. Be sure to keep the hands in front of the body to allow the freedom of stick and arm movements that is necessary to develop quick and even hand coordination.

The Timpani Sticks: Timpani sticks should have an inflexible shaft (usually of wood or aluminum) with a head of felt, cork or wood. The better sticks will have heads with wooden cores, some padding and felt coverings which are perfectly round, tightly wrapped, and without a seam. Particular attention should be paid to the absence of a seam, for a false and inferior tone will result if a seam strikes the timpani. If your present sticks have seams, draw a dark line along this seam with a Magic Marker or felt-tipped pen. Instruct your students to always play with the marked side up, thus avoiding the seam. The only problem with using a stick with marked seams is that it will tend to wear out unevenly and will have to be replaced more often. Once the felt begins to wear on the stick the resultant tone becomes unsatisfactory.

Much of the music played today varies in mood or style. The size, weight and hardness of each stick produces a different sound and the player must change sticks in order to match the character and style of each piece. If only one pair of sticks is used only the volume can be varied. The following types of sticks should be available to the timpanist:

1. Very soft, felt covered

2. General purpose, felt covered
3. Medium hard, felt covered
4. Hard, felt covered
5. Wooden head.

A soft stick produces a more legato and sonorous sound, whereas the hard stick produces a more staccato and harsh sound. The lighter in weight the stick is the thinner the tone quality is likely to be. Keeping this in mind the player should be able to achieve whatever style is necessary in his part. For example, if the part requires a soft, legato style of playing, a larger stick with soft felt covering should be used. If the part is to be soft and staccato, the better choice would be a small, hard stick with which you would play very softly. If the part is to be in a loud marcato style, the small, hard stick would not be a good choice. A larger, hard-covered stick would be needed in order to achieve the full sonority required.

Striking the Timpani: Hold the stick about three to five inches above the head, then strike the timpani with a quick flick of the wrist. After striking, the stick is drawn away from the head as if to draw the tone out of the head. When playing louder, use a stronger wrist action, raising the stick only slightly higher above the head before striking. The wrists and fingers are used almost exclusively in striking the timpano. The more the arm is used in the stroke the slower the reaction, roll and sticking technique will be because you are involving more muscles than necessary with each stroke. The primary purpose of arm motion in playing is to position the stick above the proper playing area on each head for optimum tone and resonance. The only exception to this would be a limited use of the arm when strong accented notes are required.

The stick should be parallel to the head when it strikes. This gives the best tone and resonance and will also reduce the possibilities of breaking the head while playing. The sticks should be moving straight up and down, perpendicular to the head. Avoid rolling strokes, where the stick makes a small circle within each stroke, and the sideways or glancing stroke. These types of strokes produce uneven sounding rolls, and result in unbalanced projection of sound.

The best playing area on the timpani head is located about one third of the way in from the edge to the center. When determining the playing spot remember that the larger the timpano, the further that one third distance is going to be from the edge. Always play in this area except where special effects are desired.

When playing *staccato notes* on the timpani it is generally better to use a harder stick and a good marcato stroke, and to play somewhat closer to the center of the head. The closer you strike to the center of the timpani head the less resonance there is going to be. This is what you want for staccato playing. In legato playing use a softer stick and gentle stroke. Playing closer to the edge of the head will not increase resonance, as you normally play in the area of maximum resonance. Therefore, in legato playing you should continue to strike the head in the same playing area.

The best roll on the timpani is not necessarily the fastest, but rather the one which best coincides with the speeds at which the head vibrates. The *single stroke roll* can have the controlled speed that will give the evenness of sound desired when rolling on the timpani. As a timpani head is struck it begins to vibrate. The timpani sticks must coincide with this vibration while rolling or they may strike as the head is on its upward motion. This stops the vibration momentarily and produces a "dead" spot in the roll. It is necessary, therefore, to roll more slowly on the lower pitches because the vibrations are slower. As the pitch raises and the vibrations get faster, the roll must increase in speed.

Rolls on the timpani will be indicated one of two ways— either with three lines slashed through the stem of the note as found on most snare drum music, or by the indication of a tremolo above the note or notes to be rolled. If the wavy line of the tremolo mark continues over a series of notes this should be interpreted as one continuous roll. Rolls indicated by the three slashed lines will have the notes tied together as an indication of the continuous roll. The above practice is generally used, but unfortunately not all music printed is accurate on this matter. The final decision on questionable parts must be made by looking at the other parts of the ensemble and coordinating the timpani part to fit their articulation.

The *passing roll* is a technique employed when a continuous roll changes pitch. To do this effectively the player must change from one drum to the next without stopping the rolling action. This requires fast hand and arm action to be accomplished smoothly. A good exercise to develop this is to play a series of sixteenth notes at a slow speed on each timpano without breaking the rhythm of the notes. Gradually increase the speed of these notes until they approach the speed of a roll. Passing rolls can be improved by playing in the area of the timpano closest to the other timpano to which you are moving. Care must be taken, however, to keep the sticks in the same position on the head relative to the edge and center.

One roll technique which is often poorly done on the timpani is the execution of a *forte-piano roll*. Because of the resonating quality of the timpani, the forte attack usually does not become soft enough soon enough to sound like a forte-piano roll. Instead it will sound like a forte roll with a diminuendo. This type of roll is best executed in the following manner: Strike the beginning of the roll as a single note at the desired forte level. As this tone resonates, begin the roll very softly at the edge of the timpani head. As the single forte stroke begins to die away the player will already be playing the piano roll. To the listener, the sound will be that of a continuous forte-piano roll.

Percussionists often feel that, because they are in full view of the audience, their function is to portray good showmanship. Unfortunately, one often sees wonderful examples of showmanship to the exclusion of sensible and accurate playing. The use of *cross sticking* on the timpani is a good example of this. Do not, under any circumstances, allow your timpanists to use the cross sticking technique just for the sake of a showy performance. Nothing will surpass the showmanship that results from a fine artistic and accurate performance by percussionists who are playing their instruments correctly. As when playing any of the other percussion instruments, the best practice is to alternate sticks. If, while playing, you encounter cross sticking, it would be far better to use double sticking (i.e., two lefts or two rights) and avoid the cross sticking. I have listed below some of the reasons why it is best to avoid cross sticking on the timpani:

1. There is a tendency for the stick not to strike the proper playing area of the timpani head. I have mentioned the importance of a proper body position in order to help facilitate the sticks striking the heads in the correct area. By crossing one stick over the other, the player will reduce the reach of that hand and is more likely to strike the head too close to the edge. This results in a thin, inferior tone.

2. There is the possibility of the stick handles hitting against each other or the tuning lugs of the timpani. This not only creates extraneous noises but also interferes with the rhythmic precision of the performance. Also, sticks are more likely to break when they hit the tuning lugs.

3. By cross sticking it is necessary that one hand be higher than the other in order to cross over; thus the higher stick will strike the head at a greater angle and with a longer stroke. Also, the style of timpani stick with the replaceable head often has a shaft which protrudes beyond the end of the stick, to which a nut is attached. If the player should strike the head at too great an angle this shaft may strike the head and break it.

4. Essential to good dynamic control is uniformity in the hand position, the stroke and the area of striking. All three of these factors are disturbed by the cross sticking technique. It is, therefore, almost impossible for a performer who regularly employs this technique to have good dynamic control.

Occasionally you will find a timpani part which cannot satisfactorily avoid cross sticking by the use of double sticking. By being aware of the potential problems of cross sticking the performer can make an effort to minimize them, thus retaining the tonal quality, dynamic control and rhythmic accuracy as much as possible.

The performer must be aware of the sound which is projected

to his audience. All notes played on the timpani should be uniform. I have heard performances where all the notes played with the right hand are louder than those played with the left or all the notes played on one timpano are louder than the others. This is obviously wrong but the number of players that do not pay any attention to sound projection while playing is surprising.

To avoid *unbalanced projection* be certain that each stick is raised to the same height and that the timpano is struck with the same force regardless of the hand. Not only will this keep the projection of sound balanced but it will also aid in keeping clean, accurate rhythmic patterns. Other factors which must be remembered in order to maintain a balanced projection of sound are that the higher the pitch of the timpano, the louder the notes will sound to the listener (not necessarily to the performer) and that rolls tend to sound louder then single notes when played with the same force of stroke. Therefore, rolls and higher pitched timpani should be played slightly softer to balance the projected sound.

There are two good ways to help a student become aware of sound projection. One is to have him play various exercises from lesson books at one volume level while you sit at the opposite side of the room. Each time a stroke changes volume, stop him. The other way is to use a tape recorder. Have the student play an exercise throughout at one volume level. Then play the example back so that the student can indentify the areas of unbalanced projection. You will soon find a pattern relating to the cause of this unbalanced sound.

Damping and Muting: Although these terms deal in limiting the resonance of the timpani tone, there is an important difference between them. The technique of damping (sometimes referred to as muffling) is employed to completely stop the resonance of a tone after a certain length of time. The most common application of this technique is used to prevent the timpani from ringing through a rest that might occur in the other parts of the ensemble. The technique of muting is used to soften the tone by eliminating some of the overtones and limiting the length of resonance that the tone would have.

When damping a note after it has been struck the performer should use his fingers. Holding the stick between the thumb and index finger he should use the remaining three fingers to press against the head and stop the vibrations. With a little practice this technique can be done quite noiselessly. This technique can be practiced by having the student play quarter notes alternating with quarter rests at a tempo of 60 beats per minute. Play the quarter notes with full value and in a staccato style. The damping should be done in rhythm. Have him play regular quarter notes on the first and third beats and apply the finger for damping on the second and fourth beats. When playing staccato quarter notes, play the first beat, damp on the "and" of the first beat and rest on the second beat. The student should do this first with the left hand, then the right and then alternating hands. He should learn to damp with the hand opposite the one used to play the note and with the same hand.

Damping is not always practical between notes that do not have rests in between, especially at faster tempos. Also, it may not be needed in places where the ensemble continues to play through the rests or where there is no change in the harmonic structure of the piece. In some cases it is necessary that all the timpani be damped, as the other timpani heads will start to vibrate sympathetically while playing. Lightly touching each timpani head with the techniques described above will stop the resonance of all the heads. A better solution, however, if you are not going to be using all of your timpani in a particular number is to place a piece of weighted felt cloth used for muting on the head to prevent it from responding to the sympathetic vibrations.

A performer may mute the timpani in two ways. One way is to place a small mute of weighted felt on the head while playing. This mute can be made with a piece of felt sewn around some sort of padding and a weight. When making these attach two long cords or straps and tie the mutes to one of the tuning lugs of the timpani. This way the mutes are always available to the player. For the minimum amount of muting, place the mute in the center of the head and gradually move it toward the edge of the head to increase the muting effect.

Another way of muting, if the passage is not complex, is to play with one hand and use the fingers of the other hand to act as the mute. The positioning of the hand for muting would be the same as that employed with the felt mutes, with the additional ability to control the amount of muting by the amount of pressure exerted by the fingers. This technique is very convenient if you have just a short section of a piece which needs to be muted.

The term "coperto" will often be seen to indicate the need for a mute. Do not confuse this with the term "muta" which is the Italian word indicating a change of pitch. Muting may also be used even though not marked in the music whenever you need to play softer or wish to reduce the reasonance of the timpani tone.

Tuning the Timpani: Because the timpani is tuned to a specific pitch, playing *in tune* should be the primary objective of the timpanist and the focal point in his training.

The method which I recommend for tuning is one which employs the humming of the pitch and the principle of sympathetic vibrations. Have the student play the required note on the pitchpipe and then hum this pitch into the timpano head while moving the pedal or tuning handle slowly upwards. When the head is at the same pitch as the hum, sympathetic vibrations will cause the head to "hum" back. Because of the overtones involved the head will "hum" at some pitches other than the one being hummed, so be certain that the head is sounding the exact same pitch. The advantages to this method of tuning are that the pitch will be more accurate and it is a silent way of tuning as it does not require the player to hit the head to find the pitch. This method does require that the timpanist be able to match pitches (a skill which is often not developed among young timpani players) and hum at a constant pitch.

In another method of tuning, the player strikes the head lightly with the timpani stick or fingers and adjusts the pedal until the proper pitch is achieved. There are a few common problems with this method of tuning which I think make it undesirable. First, the tapping of the timpani, no matter how softly, can often be heard by the audience and the ensemble.

Also, the louder the ensemble plays, the louder the timpanist must tap in order to hear his pitch. Secondly, by tapping *lightly* the timpanist will not produce a true fundamental pitch but rather will hear mainly the overtones. If you tune to the overtones the fundamental pitch, which will sound when the timpani is struck in a normal fashion, may be out of tune. Hence no matter how carefully the timpanist tunes, there is a very good chance he will be out of tune when he begins to play.

As you release the pedal or tuning handle the head will not always return fully to the original position. When you begin to play, the head returns to this position and the tone will go flat. This will happen only when you are tuning down to a lower pitch. It can be avoided by going *below* the desired pitch and pressing into the center of the head before tuning up to the note you want.

Unless the player has perfect pitch, he will always need to rely upon something to give him a starting pitch and to check pitches through the process of the rehearsal. The pitchpipe is best for this as other instruments such as a piano, bells, and marimba, may not always be available and often tend to be too loud for this purpose. Under no circumstances should the player rely upon tuning gauges which are found on some timpani. These gauges can only serve as a visual guide to the professional doing complex tuning and must be set by ear before each performance. The main reason I am against the tuning gauge is that the student timpanist must develop his own aural ability and this will not happen if he depends upon the tuning gauge.

If the timpani parts do not come with the starting pitches indicated it is a good idea for the player to mark the starting pitches needed. This makes it much easier to tune the timpani when starting without having to look through the piece to determine the pitches required. Also, as tuning changes occur within a piece the new pitch should be indicated in writing prior to the change. I would advise that the player mark in the music the exact changes needed at the point where he should begin to tune. I do this by indicating both the present pitch and new pitch needed. This keeps the player better orientated as to what pitches are on which timpani and reminds him of the interval between the two pitches when retuning. In very complex parts where there is an excessive amount of tuning changes, I indicate the pitches on each timpano at the beginning of each major or easily recognizable section within the piece. During long rests it is a good idea to mark cues into the rests so you can find your place after retuning.

The Aural Development of the Timpanist: Good aural ability is essential in a timpanist. Ear training and the development of tuning skills on the timpani are really the most difficult aspects of the timpanist's training and can only be developed if approached very positively by the director and included as a part of every lesson. The primary skill which the timpanist needs to develop is the ability to match pitches, identify intervals, sing them, and tune the timpani to these intervals. The student must be able to mentally hold the pitch despite the ensemble playing other notes or even in other keys.

The first step would be to train your timpanists to match pitches. This is most easily done by playing notes on the piano and having them hum the pitch. After the student is able to match pitches successfully (this would also include pitches that fall outside his vocal range) he should begin to sing both scales and simple intervals in this order: octaves, fourths, fifths, thirds, sixths, seconds and sevenths. The intervals should be sung both up and down. This is not always easily done but this portion of the training should not be underestimated, for it is the crux of the whole aural development program.

After the student is able to sing the above intervals he should begin to work on more abstract intervals. For this purpose I have developed a card system which will present the student with every interval possibility on the timpani. Starting with only two timpani, make a set of cards for each timpano listing every possible note available on that timpano. (For example, the 26" timpano would have one card for each of the following pitches: B^b, C^b, C, $C^\#$, D^b, D, $D^\#$, E^b, E, $E^\#$, F^b F, $F^\#$, G^b, G.) Mix up the cards within each set and place them on a pile face up. Have the student tune the timpani to the two notes showing on the top of the piles. Now turn over one card at a time and have the student sing the interval between the old and new note and tune that particular timpano to the new pitch. Check the results with a piano and adjust if necessary. Repeat this sequence with a card from the other pile. This procedure can later be made more difficult by turning one card on each pile at the same time, using three or four sets of cards for each of three or four timpani, setting a time limit for the tuning changes and finally having the student count a certain number of beats while tuning. This training will prepare him for almost any possibility that might arise in music and will certainly make the easier tuning changes much simpler for him.

Another problem the timpanist will encounter is that no matter how well he can tune in a lesson or by himself, he cannot seem to do as well when the ensemble is playing. One practice that might help is to play records or a radio while tuning to help the student learn to maintain the pitch regardless of other sounds around him.

5

How to Teach the Snare Drum Through Total Percussion

The Snare Drum and its Relationship to the
Total Percussion

Traditionally the snare drum has been the foundation in the training of most percussionists. In many cases it has also been the extent of that training as well. If we are to develop total percussionists, we must place the snare drum in its proper perspective as part of the total percussion. In developing a total percussion program this may well prove to be the greatest obstacle encountered. We have placed such emphasis on the snare drum, to the exclusion of most of the other percussion instruments, that many of our students now feel that being a percussionist means to play the snare drum. I have known good students who wanted to play the "drums." They did a fine job while studying the snare drum, but as soon as the timpani or the bells were introduced into the lesson plan they "turned off" and lost interest in playing. It is not surprising that, after learning to play the snare drum, they did not want to start over by learning to read notes, identify pitches, play scales or study

83

the various nuances that are available from all the percussion instruments, even though these are essential in the training of the percussionist. For this reason I now start all percussion students in the total percussion and not just on snare drum. From the beginning they are taught to play the snare drum, timpani and mallet percussion. They learn from the start that they must be responsible for all three of these instrument areas plus the many "accessory" instruments which comprise the percussion family.

I do not feel that the primary objective of a student's training on snare drum should be limited to the ability to play class "A" solos and perform the twenty-six rudiments. The student should be taught to play the snare drum in an intelligent and musical manner while developing an understanding of complex rhythmic patterns. The study of the rudiments and rudimental solos should be used as a technique builder which develops usable skills but not as the ultimate achievement in the area of snare drum training. By incorporating the mallet percussion and timpani along with the snare drum training there is bound to be a carryover of the musical aspect of playing and these areas should be stressed when teaching the total percussion.

Ideally the student should know all the rudiments and when to use them before entering high school. He should also have an understanding of the four styles of rolls used on the snare drum (i.e., single stroke, rudimental, concert and press rolls) and when they are used. He should know where and how to strike the snare drum, and should be able to tune his drum for optimum sound and projection. I have not said he should be completely accomplished in each of these areas, but rather should have the basic knowledge and at least elementary skill in each area. These skills are then perfected and extended during the high school years.

Any percussionist must have a strong, dependable knowledge of rhythm and must be steady and reliable as a keeper of the tempo. The study of the snare drum best contributes to these qualities, as one of the basic skills to be developed is that of rhythmic understanding. Where the mallet percussion stresses melodic playing and the timpani stresses aural development, the snare drum will stress rhythmic knowledge. All three areas are important for the total percussionist and this knowledge is essential if he is to contribute musically as a member of an ensemble.

Physical Characteristics of the Snare Drum

Photo courtesy of Rogers Drums

Picture 5–1.

Construction: The snare drum consists of a cylindrical shell made of metal or wood covered at each end by a batter head or a snare head. The metal shell can best produce the type of snare drum sound which is desirable in the concert situation as it will tend to project a crisper sound. This means clearly articulated rhythms and a responsive snare sound while playing.

Size: For most concert work the drum should be either fourteen or fifteen inches in diameter with a depth of from five to eight inches. I recommend a 6½" x 14" drum for general use; however, the following should be kept in mind.

A larger snare drum is capable of greater volume but is also less sensitive in response as it involves a larger air column. This requires larger sticks, thicker heads and heavier snares to produce a good sound. The smaller drum is going to be more responsive and crisper in sound but have less projection power. One must also consider the size of the performance room and the size and type of ensemble when deciding on the proper size snare drum to use. If you have a large group or are playing in a large hall you will probably need the volume of the larger size snare drum. If your group is small or is playing chamber type music the smaller drum is necessary. Because your needs will vary according to the music you play it is a good idea to have a variety of snare drum sizes available. When purchasing snare drum, therefore, do not buy three or four drums that are matched in size. Never use a snare drum larger than an eight by fifteen inch for indoor concert work and especially avoid the use of field drums or marching drums for concert snare drum work unless specifically called for in the music.

The Snares: The three basic types of snares made are wire, gut and nylon. These come in a variety of combinations and sizes which offers a large choice of snares for the player. Although some of these snares are best suited for the marching drums I shall mention them here for the sake of comparison.

Perhaps the most common snare used in concert work is the wire snare. This is a spiraled wire which rests against the snare head. It is the most sensitive of the snares and for this reason the most practical for concert use. Wire snares with from ten to fourteen strands will produce the best sound. Snare strands are available with up to twenty strands although these are more commonly used in dance drum sets. In many cases, the choice of snares will be limited to those that fit on your particular model snare drum.

The gut snare has a characteristically full tone which responds best at loud volumes. It is most commonly found on field drums. It is not as sensitive as the wire snare and therefore has particularly poor sound when played softly. For this reason I do not recommend the exclusive use of gut snares for concert playing, especially on the size snare drums that I recommend. The gut snare, being a natural material, is also affected by the humidity and must always be adjusted before and after each use.

The nylon snare is a more recent development and an improvement upon the gut snare. It is not affected by the humidity and is somewhat more responsive than the gut snare in softer playing while still being capable of producing a good, full tone at loud volumes. I recommend this type of snare for field drums. There are some who use nylon snares on concert snare drums. I do not recommend this as they are still not responsive enough for the delicate playing often required. If you wish to have a fuller sound from your snare drum without loosing the sensitivity needed in softer parts, I suggest using a combination of the wire and nylon snares at the ratio of two wire strands to each nylon strand.

For better tone and longer life the snares should remain under the same tension at all times regardless of whether they are on or off the snare head. This type of snare strainer is usually called a "duel" or "parallel" snare release. Most snare strainers, however, release the tension on the snare when it is removed from the snare head. For optimum tone the snares should cover the entire surface of the snare head.

Unequal tension of the snares is one of the greatest causes of poor snare sound and a "buzzy" ring while playing. If any of the snares have less tension on them they will vibrate for a longer time than the others, causing this "buzzy" sound. Some manufacturers produce snare strainers which allow for the individual adjustment of the tension on each snare. If you do not have this adjustment available you should replace the entire snare unit or cut off the few single strands that are stretched out of shape.

The Snare Drum Heads: There are two types of heads used on the snare drum. The batter head, which is used on top, is thicker and stronger to enable it to withstand the striking of the sticks. The snare head, which is on the bottom, is much thinner and much more sensitive. When the batter head is struck it activates the air column within the drum which in turn sets the snare head in motion. This motion is transferred to the snare which produces the snare sound. Because the snare head is so thin it should never be used as a batter head. The reverse is also true in that the batter head is too thick and unresponsive to react well as a snare head. For best tone, therefore, it is important to use the proper head in the proper location.

Snare drum heads are made of either calfskin or plastic. The calfskin head is affected by humidity and will change tension with the weather, will need to be adjusted before each playing and will need to have the collar reset on occasion. Plastic heads, on the other hand, are not noticeably affected by the weather, have a built-in collar which will hold, and once the head is in place and adjusted, should not have to be changed. Because of the consistency and ease of maintenance offered by the plastic head and the fact that there is little difference in the tone produced, I recommend its use on snare drums.

When choosing a plastic batter head, be sure to choose one which has a rough surface. Some players feel that the smooth surface of some plastic heads does not produce as good a response to the sticks as they strike the head. Also, you will not be able to get a good sliding brush sound from this head. One company makes a spray which can be applied to the head to make it rough.

The Snare Drum Sticks: In selecting sticks to use on the snare drum one factor which is often overlooked is the size of drum upon which they will be used. The size of the stick must correspond with the size of the snare drum. By using the correct size stick you will receive the best tonal response and stick control from your drum. This can be illustrated if you try to play a field drum with thin dance drum sticks. You would find that it is virtually impossible to produce any sound this way let alone a good field drum sound. Likewise, if you try to play the dance drums with heavy marching drum sticks you will have little control over stick coordination and volume and will be unable to play rapid rhythm patterns delicately. If extreme variations in stick and drum sizes make a difference, so will the lesser variations that you are more likely to encounter.

A good choice for general concert work on a six-and-a-half by fifteen inch drum would be either a #2A or #2B. If you have a snare drum which is eight inches deep try going to a slightly heavier stick. The reverse would be true if your drum depth was less than six-and-a-half inches.

Sticks should be free from warping. This can easily be checked by rolling each stick along a flat surface. The sticks should also be of equal weight and density. The weight you can feel just by holding them in each hand and the density can be checked by tapping the sticks against a hard surface such as a piece of metal or the tile floor. If the density is similar the sticks will have a similar sound. The sticks that you choose should have a heavier shoulder for durability. These factors are essential if you wish to achieve a balanced sound in your snare drum playing.

Some sticks are now made with nylon tips which produce a better tone when using them on cymbals. These sticks are especially useful in dance drum use. Unfortunately, the addition of a nylon tip does not give the strength of a complete stick turned out of wood. My experience has been that this stick tends to break more easily in concert playing. Another new style of stick is one made of laminated wood. This stick is usually free of warps and is generally well balanced. My experience with this stick has been that it also breaks more easily than the solid hickory stick. Nothing can surpass a well balanced, warp-free stick of this type.

Under no circumstances should you use sticks which are broken, cracked, chipped or split. The response from these sticks will not be the same even if the cracked or broken part is temporarily repaired.

The Snare Drum Stand: It is hard to understand why a school will invest money in a fine snare drum and then place it on a stand which is both unstable and inoperative. A drum can be damaged very easily when it falls off of a stand. Good snare drum stands are well worth the cost as they provide good support to the snare drum. The stand should be easily adjustable to a height of at least thirty-six inches from the floor. The angle of the drum should also be adjustable. The set screws used for these adjustments should set firmly so that there is no chance of coming loose. The arms which hold the drum should be non-flexible but adjustable to fit the drum's diameter. If these arms can bend easily there is a chance that the drum head and/or snares will rest on the stand. This not only impedes sound but is also likely to cause both head and snare damage. When placing the drum on the stand at an angle, be certain that the sliding arm is on the high side. If this arm should then come loose it cannot drop the drum as the weight of the drum would be on the lower two arms.

The Practice Pad: The practice pad is commonly used at home for the student's practice, eliminating the need for buying a drum and making the practice sessions quieter. It is important that the practice pad simulate the action of the snare drum head as closely as possible. It should produce a good rebound similar to that of the snare drum and be easily heard by the player when practicing. I recommend a tunable drum pad with a plastic head; however, the instructor may wish to try a few different models to see which best suits his needs before ordering them for his students.

There is another style pad made for the student who owns a drum but finds that it is sometimes too loud to practice around the house. This is a large rubber pad which covers the full head surface of the snare drum and in effect muffles the drum.

Practice pads should be mounted on a stand or placed on a table so that they will be at the correct height.

Practicing on a drum pad can be an important part of the snare drummer's training and should always be used as part of the practice and lesson routine. The practice pad is especially useful when learning the rudiments and rolls as the imperfections can be more easily heard. On the snare drum, many of the inaccuracies are covered up by the resonance of the drum; on the pad there is no resonance and every beat can easily be heard.

The Maintenance of the Snare Drum

Care of the Snare Drum: Proper care of the heads and snares is the primary job in the care of your snare drum. Heads should be cleaned when necessary. Plastic heads are far easier to maintain, which is another reason why I prefer them over calfskin heads. They can be wiped regularly with warm water and a damp cloth. For stubborn stains remove the head from the drum and scrub with a stiff brush and kitchen cleanser, rinse and dry thoroughly, then replace. Be certain to carefully adjust the head tension when resetting the head on the drum. Calfskin heads can be cleaned with cool water, a mild hand soap and a clean cloth. Use only a damp, soapy cloth when cleaning and avoid getting the flesh hoop wet or allowing water to stand on the head. Wipe off the soap and dirt with another clean damp cloth. Allow the head to dry overnight before playing on it. Calfskin heads should not be cleaned as often as plastic heads.

Wire snares should not be pulled, plucked or strummed either individually or collectively as this spiraled wire is easily stretched. Once a snare has stretched, it is impossible to adjust it for a good snare drum sound. If you have any snares that are stretched you can either replace the entire set or cut off those particular snares. (This, of course, should not be done too often.)

Snare drums should not be stored in an area of direct heat from a register or in front of windows. It would be best to cover the drum when not in use and store in its own compartment in a drum cabinet or in a fiber case. When storing the drum in a case, do not pack any other loose equipment into the case with it. Store the drum on its stand only if it is in an area which is free from all traffic. It is very easy to have a snare drum knocked off the stand by a passing individual.

Head Adjustment: As in the timpani, the tension on the snare drum heads must be balanced. An unbalanced head will produce a different response from the sticks as they strike the head and will affect the evenness of sound which results. Also, the unbalanced head does not vibrate evenly when struck. This causes the head to counteract its own vibrations resulting in an inferior sound as the tone cancels itself out. Check the snare drum head for balance by tapping it lightly alongside of each tuning lug while holding the other head against a soft cloth to prevent it from vibrating. Work for the same pitch at each point.

When placing a new head on a snare drum be certain that there are no loose particles inside the drum and that there is no dirt on the rim. Place the head on the drum, mount the counter hoop and secure the lugs evenly to eliminate the wrinkles from the head. After doing this, press down in the center of the head to set it against the rim. With the snares off, begin to tune the drum head as described above.

Calfskin heads must be kept loose after playing in damp weather and tight after playing in dry weather. This will require a resetting of both heads before and after each playing session. The calfskin head will also need an occasional resetting of the collar. This would be done in the same manner as described for timpani heads in Chapter 4.

Playing Techniques for the Snare Drum

Adjusting the Snare Drum Sound: The current preference for a snare drum sound is a crisp, high-pitched sound free from extra vibrations or rattles. The adjustment of the head and snare to the proper tension is vital in producing this sound. If the heads are adjusted too loosely the sound will not have a distinct rhythmic clarity and the sticks will not have good rebound action. Conversely, if the heads are adjusted too tightly the sound will be too ringy and will lack good snare response and depth of tone. Also, there will be too much rebound action by the sticks for good control.

Two thoughts now prevail regarding the head tension in achieving the proper sound from your snare drum. Some believe that the batter head should be tighter than the snare head and others feel just the opposite. I suggest you try both ways and determine which sound you prefer. Regardless of which method you prefer, however, it is most important that you adjust the tension of the batter head first in order to achieve a good tension for stick rebound and coordination as you play.

Another factor which is important in the snare drum sound is the snare adjustment. Set the snare strainer throw in the "on" position and loosen the adjustment knob until the snares are completely away from the head. Then tap lightly with one stick while you slowly tighten the adjustment knob. Continue this until the sound is crisp and free from any ringing from the head.

It will be necessary when adjusting your drum to muffle it slightly to remove some of the ringing. There are three methods of muffling this ringing. One is to use the internal muffler, if available, on your drum. This should be used sparingly and usually needs only to be set with a slight pressure on the head. If set at the full muffle position too much of the resonance will be removed, thus reducing the quality of tone. The second way to muffle is to place a strip of cloth across the rim of the drum before placing the batter head on the drum. The batter head will hold the cloth in place and the cloth will act as a muffler. The problem with this method is that it may muffle too much and there is no way that you can adjust this without removing the head and moving the cloth more toward the edge of the drum. The third way to muffle is to place a piece of moleskin (available at any drugstore) on the head. This is an especially effective means of muffling tenor drums and tom toms that do not have a bottom head as it can be placed on the underside of the head. The moleskin has an adhesive backing and can be moved to different positions on the head to vary the amount of muffling you might want for different numbers. The closer the moleskin is placed to the center or edge of the head, the less it will muffle.

The Grip: Currently there is much discussion regarding the pros and cons of the traditional snare drum grip and the matched grip. I advocate the use of the matched grip because the same muscles of each hand are being developed. Also, this grip can be used for playing the snare drum, timpani, mallet percussion and many of the accessory percussion instruments as well. This makes more sense than trying to develop three separate stick grips, each of which needs different muscle coordination.

Regarding this muscle coordination, Gene Pollart wrote an article in the *Percussionist* in which he stated:

> The matched grip involves more coordination of the participating muscles, has more potential power at its disposal to help control the action or movement, and because of its simple movement and more potential power, it will produce more sustained endurance.[1]

---

[1] Gene Pollart, "A Study of Muscle Efficiency in Comparing the Matched Grip and the Traditional Grip," *Percussionist*, Vol. IV, No. 4 (May, 1967), p. 184.

Mr. Pollart reached this conclusion after an intensive study of the muscles involved in both types of snare drum grips.

Regarding the advantages of teaching the matched grip to your students, Forrest Clark wrote the following in an article regarding the two styles of snare drum grips:

> For those who are largely involved with teaching, I can certainly recommend the matched grip as a technique which is far easier to comprehend, far easier to teach and far easier to learn. The beginner . . . is able to spend more of his concentration upon the musical aspects of his training instead of upon the usual mechanical problems presented by the traditional left-hand grip.[2]

The matched grip is the same as the two mallet grip described in the chapter on the mallet percussion and the same used in playing the timpani. The hand must be parallel to the floor with the palm facing down. The hand moves primarily from the wrist which should be from six to eight inches in front of the body. Elbows should be hanging freely to the side about two to three inches from the body with the forearms pointing inwards. The sticks will meet at about a 90 degree angle to the drum head. For the actual hand grip see the grip for xylophone mallets in Chapter 3.

The Stance: When the snare drum is used in concert playing it should always be played from a standing position. The reason for this is that oftentimes the drummer needs to move to other instruments in his area and it is to his advantage to be standing. Also, it is difficult to achieve the proper hand and arm positions while sitting. The player should stand in a comfortable position with the feet spaced slightly apart and one foot slightly ahead of the other to help maintain balance. The body weight should be distributed over both feet with slightly more weight on the forward foot. This tends to create more aggressive playing. The player should stand about twelve inches from the drum. This distance will allow the sticks to strike the proper playing area of

---

[2]Forrest Clark, "Pros and Cons of Matched Grip Snare Drumming," *Percussionist*, Vol. VI, No. 3 (March, 1969), p. 85.

the drum when the hands are extended from six to eight inches from the body.

The Drum Position: When using the matched grip the snare drum should be slightly below waist level and parallel to the floor. The snare strainer release should be located near the player so that it is easily available while playing. When using a drum pad for practice it is important that it also be slightly below waist level so that a proper development of the grips will ensue. If the drum pad has a built-in angle, position it so that the high side is away from the player.

Striking the Drum: The best place to strike the snare drum for normal playing is directly above the snares in an area between the center and edge of the head. By playing directly above the snares you will achieve a more direct response by the snares to the stick striking the batter head. Strike halfway between the center and the edge of the head because this is the area of greatest vibration. The tone which results from striking in this area will have the best quality.

The angle of the sticks should be just high enough to avoid hitting the rim of the drum. If your drum is at the proper height this will also produce the best hand position for playing.

The stroke used should be the same as that used on the mallet percussion and timpani. Draw the tone out of the drum, do not pound it in. This is done by starting each stroke near the head, striking with a quick flick of the wrist and lifting the stick away from the head. Return the stick to this position before the next note. Only the wrists should be involved in this action and any vertical movement of the forearm should be avoided except in extremely loud playing. Accents are played by using greater wrist action, but not more arm action. Bring the stick tip farther back before striking the drum and use a greater force in the flick of the wrist action. It is important to avoid the use of the arm in this stroke as this will cause a loss of stick control. In order to achieve the best possible sound from the snare drum good stick control along with proper arm and hand movements are essential.

It is best for the beginner to alternate his hands at all times while playing. The exceptions to this are certain rudiments which are sticked otherwise. This is necessary in order to develop equal control in both hands. If you allow the student to favor a certain hand, he will develop in this hand a greater degree of coordination than in the other and will then have difficulty in playing evenly, especially in the rolls.

I do not advocate the "Straight System" or right-hand lead system of playing. My objection to this system is that it will develop the strength and coordination of the right hand over that of the left hand. If you wish to use this system, however, I suggest that it be employed after the student has advanced past the area of developing equal hand coordination. Advanced students will often find that they can play a succession of single notes or other rhythmic patterns much more evenly by using only one hand. This technique is perfectly proper at the advanced stage, but should not be taught to the beginning student.

The Rim Shot: The rim shot is a technique often called for in drum parts which can be played in three ways. What was originally intended by this instruction was to strike the drum head and rim at the same time with the sticks. Unfortunately, most student percussionists will miss either the rim or the head and, therefore, the rim shot. It is a difficult technique to execute in this manner because the drum must always be at the same height and angle and have the same size collar. The rim shot can also be played by either placing one stick against the head and striking it on the shaft with the other or by laying one stick against the drum head *and rim* and striking it with the other. Although not as pure a sound, either method is much more dependable. Neither method can be used, however, in situations where a rim shot is called for in fast playing.

The Roll: The roll on the snare drum is a fundamental technique since it is the only means in which the player can sustain a sound. For this reason all rolls must be one continuous sound and not a multitude of fast notes. Rolls are perhaps the most difficult aspect of playing the snare drum and will take a number of years to develop properly. The instructor should realize this and consider slow progress with proper hand coordination and stick control as essential to the ultimate end.

Many band directors do not seem to realize that there are many types and styles of rolls which must be used under different playing conditions. Each of those rolls is executed in a different manner.

Although the *Single Stroke Roll* is considered a roll in the listing of rudiments it does not fall in the same category as the other rolls. The single stroke roll when played rapidly may sound like one continuous sound, but its purpose is a rapid succession of individual strokes. The single stroke roll is played with a single stroke from each hand while alternating. The alternating of the sticks for this roll serves as a good developmental exercise for the hand-to-hand technique, muscle coordination and strength needed on the snare drum.

The Rudimental Roll is also known as the military, parade, double-bounce or open roll. This roll is most commonly suited to military music and marching and should *not* be used regularly in concert playing. Unfortunately, most young drum students learn this roll when beginning and are never taught any other style of roll. Because of this we hear too much use of the rudimental roll in high school concert pieces that are neither marches nor in a military style.

The rudimental roll is performed with a stroke-bounce technique. The hand moves from the wrist and makes one stroke when striking the drum and the fingers apply pressure to the stick causing it to bounce *once* before the hand draws the sticks away from the head. When playing the rudimental roll correctly, you should be able to discern the individual beats within the roll which, when played at a march tempo, should produce the rhythm of 32nd notes.

The rudimental roll technique plays an active part in the playing of many of the twenty-six rudiments. The following rudiments, for example, are derived from the rudimental roll: Long roll, five-stroke roll, seven-stroke roll, nine-stroke roll, ten-stroke roll, eleven-stroke roll, thirteen-stroke roll, fifteen-stroke roll and seventeen-stroke roll. Also, the action of the stroke-bounce technique is employed in the ruff, single drag, double drag, single ratamacue, double ratamacue, triple ratamacue, paradiddle, drag paradiddle and lesson 25. For this reason the study of the rudimental roll is essential to the training of the students. Further discussion of the rudimental roll and the rudiments can be found in Chapter 8 dealing with the marching percussion.

The *Concert Style Roll* is also known as the multiple-bounce or closed roll and is the style roll which should be more commonly used in concert work. When performing this roll the hand should make one stroke from the wrist, and the finger then applies slight pressure to the stick and allows it to bounce *more than once.* The initial stroke and its multiple bounces are again the result of a single wrist action in the hand. In this style roll there should not be any discernible beats as in the rudimental roll. Each stroke should produce either two or three bounces. Each hand must produce the same number of bounces in order to maintain an even sound. Unlike the rudimental roll there is no set number of pulsations required per beat, thus it can easily be played at any tempo. (The rudimental roll cannot be played at slow speeds as the 32nd notes would become too slow to execute properly.)

The Press Roll is also called the jazz roll or forced-bounce roll. This style roll is most common in dance drum playing and not often applicable to concert work. The press roll, unlike the other rolls, is not based upon the stroke-bounce or stroke multiple-bounce technique. Instead of an initial stroke, the press roll is started by pressing both sticks on the head at the same time. The resultant sound of the press roll will not have much resonance because the pressure action reduces the vibrations of the head. Press rolls generally start with an accent and have a soft release.

Any of the three styles of rolls listed above can be used in concert work if the number being performed is in the particular style in which the roll fits. Regardless of the style of roll used, however, there are a few guidelines which should be followed for maintaining an even sounding roll:

1) Most important is to have both hands playing the same style roll. Be sure that the number and style of bounces in each hand are the same while playing. As obvious as this might sound, careful observation of your students' rolls may reveal that this is not happening.

2) The stroke and its bounce(s) should be the same volume. Most beginning players start with a stroke which is much louder than the succeeding bounces and often they never improve upon this. If the initial stroke is louder than the bounce(s) the resulting roll will always be uneven.

3) Both hands should strike at the same volume. Of course you should avoid having one hand louder than the other in any percussion playing, but this fault becomes much more noticeable when playing the roll. Again, the use of the matched grip will help this as both hands are using the same muscle action, therefore making it easier to maintain equal control of the height and force of each stroke.

4) Both sticks should strike at the same distance from the rim. Different areas of the snare drum head will produce different sounds. If you play a roll with each stick on a different area of the head the resultant roll will be uneven.

5) Play with both sticks directly above the snares. A different sound will also result from a stroke which is played above the snares as opposed to one which is not.

6) Both sticks should strike the head at the same angle as a variance in the angle will affect both the volume and the rebound action.

The percussionist should learn to play all three styles of rolls described with the accents at both the beginning and the end of the roll. Where the accent should be played is not always indicated in the music but can be determined by the location of the beat. If the roll begins on a strong beat of the measure the accent would probably be at the beginning. If the roll ends on the strong beat, the accent would probably come at the end. Exceptions to this would occur in syncopated rhythms and in cases where no accent would be wanted. In most cases, by carefully listening to the articulation and rhythm of the rest of the ensemble it becomes quite apparent where the accents should lie.

6

How to Teach the Accessory Percussion Instruments Through Total Percussion

In this chapter I list the most commonly used "accessory" percussion instruments, give a brief description of their construction and explain how to play them. There is much a player needs to know about each of these instruments in order to obtain the best sound, clean rhythmic articulation and the dynamic control which are essential for a good musical performance. These are musical instruments, not simply objects to be struck, and each requires special instruction on how to be played. Do not allow students to play any of these instruments without first explaining the playing techniques required for each. Most percussionists should be able to develop the technique required quite easily as all relate to the basic stroke and wrist action used for the snare drum, timpani or mallet percussion.

I have described the usual means of playing each of the instruments and these techniques should be used most of the time. All of these instruments are also open to experimentation for different sound effects if so desired, but I believe that the student should have the basic playing technique and resultant sound of each instrument in mind before trying to discover new sounds.

The Bass Drum

Photo courtesy of Ludwig Industries
Picture 6–1.

The bass drum is the foundation of your percussion section and of your entire ensemble and should not be underestimated. I'm sure tha most band directors realize that a poor bass drummer can destroy the entire ensemble's unity and rhythmic drive. Yet we often find that the weakest player in the percussion section is placed on the bass drum because he might not be capable of handling anything else. Not only does this defeat the program of teaching the total percussion, but it also works against the entire ensemble. A well trained, sensitive percussionist playing the bass drum in a musical manner can be one of the greatest assets of your ensemble. I do not advocate putting your best percussionist on bass drum and having him play nothing else, for this also is contrary to the principle of teaching total percussion. I am suggesting, rather, that you train all your percussionists to be good bass drummers by providing an understanding of the instrument, its capabilities and responsibilities, and by giving each one the experience of playing the bass drum.

Physical Characteristics of the Bass Drum

*Construction—*The bass drum shell is generally made of wood with a head on both sides. The heads should be of equal thickness and can be either calfskin or plastic. I recommend the plastic head for the bass drum as this large a calfskin head will be greatly affected by the humidity.

Bass drums are available with either single or separate tension. The single tension style has just one tuning rod or lug to tighten both heads of the bass drum. This is not a desirable feature as it prevents adjusting the tension of one head independently of the other. Therefore, I recommend the separate-tension style bass drum as the only suitable one.

The use of mechanical mufflers which are attached to the rim ·of the bass drum and rest against the outside of the head should be avoided. These mufflers reduce the resonance, thus affecting the quality of the tone. They also prevent flexibility in the amount of muffling required and strongly limit the ability of the bass drummer to differentiate between styles of playing.

Size—Concert bass drums range in size from 14" x 28" to 18" x 40" or occasionally even larger. The 16" x 36" size is the most common and I recommend this size for most concert playing. If you have an exceptionally small group you might be able to use a slightly smaller size, but if the bass drum is too small it will lose the low bass sound. Likewise, a larger size drum might be suitable for a very large ensemble but if it becomes too large the tone will lose its resonant quality. If cost is a factor when purchasing a bass drum, you can save money by compromising on the choice of finish rather than on the size. A bass drum with a lacquered shell will sound just as good as one with a pearl finish, but might cost from $25.00 to $50.00 less.

The Beaters—Most commercially made bass drum beaters are satisfactory, but there should be a choice of size, weight and hardness available to the player. You should have four pairs of beaters. I list them below in the order most needed so that you can add these gradually if you need to:

1. one pair, medium-soft lamb's wool
2. one pair, hard felt
3. one pair, medium-hard lamb's wool
4. one pair, wood

Always purchase bass drum beaters in pairs so they will be available for rolling. Never roll on the bass drum with just one double-end beater. Using timpani sticks for rolling is not a good idea as often they are too light to produce a desirable tone on the bass drum.

The Stand—There are essentially two styles of bass drum stands available. One is the metal folding stand and the other is a tilting frame to which the bass drum is attached. No matter which style of stand you choose, it must be sturdy, well padded, free from rattles and have rubber feet or casters with good locks to prevent the drum from moving while playing. A height adjustment is also necessary as different size bass drums need to be held at different heights. On the tilting stands the height adjustment is not as important, as these stands are constructed to hold only certain size bass drums. I recommend the tilting bass drum stand for it can provide much better access to the bass drum when rolls are required, thus contributing toward better sounding rolls. These stands are, however, considerably more expensive than the conventional folding stands and I realize that many schools may not be able to afford them. In this case a folding stand is satisfactory providing it is sturdy, well padded and adjustable.

Playing the Bass Drum

The Stance—Stand behind and to the right of the bass drum. This will position you for playing on the right-hand head. The left hand should be available for placement on the left head for muffling. When muffling of the right head is desired, the right foot should be placed upon a low box or stool located to the right of the drum which will position the right knee just slightly off center on the head. The right foot need be placed on this stool only when certain muffling conditions are required.

The Grip—The grip used to hold the bass drum beater is essentially the same as that used for the snare drum, timpani or mallet percussion. The only difference is that the palm of the right hand faces the bass drum head. If you have the double-end bass drum beater, better balance will be achieved if you hold this on the wooden handle and not on the lamb's-wool end.

The Stroke—The type of stroke used in playing the base drum is the same as that used on any of the other percussion instruments. Hold the beater about three to four inches away from the head and strike with the quick "flick of the wrist" concept drawing the beater away from the head after striking as if to draw the tone out of the head. Some motion of the forearm will be necessary with this stroke as this is a large instrument and the stroke must also be somewhat larger. There are some who advocate the use of a glancing stroke when playing the bass drum but I do not feel this type of stroke produces the full resonant tone desired. I recommend a direct stroke which approaches the head at a 90 degree angle for the best tonal results.

The head should be struck slightly off center for most playing. When playing in a staccato style you can strike closer to the center but this will result in a loss of tone quality. Staccato playing can be accomplished much better by muffling both heads (left hand and right knee as described earlier) and continuing to play in the same general playing area. Take care not to press the heads too hard while muffling as you will lose the low, resonant quality of the bass drum. For more legato playing, remove the muffling hand and knee from each head and strike about halfway between the center and edge.

Rolling on the Bass Drum—Bass drum rolls should never be attempted with a double-end beater. You cannot produce an even roll this way as you are, in essence, using two different size beaters not to mention the problems of wrist coordination involved. For this reason I recommend that all bass drum beaters be purchased in pairs and that all bass drum rolls be performed with two beaters. Use both beaters on the same head when rolling. If you have a bass drum stand which tilts you will be able to use the matched grip. If your bass drum stand does not tilt, the rudimental snare drum grip will work quite well if your players are familiar with this grip. The matched grip may also be used but it will be necessary to lean over the bass drum somewhat in order to reach the head easily. Do not use any form of muffling when playing the roll.

Tuning the Bass Drum—The bass drum should have a low, indefinite pitch. If your bass drum is being tuned to a specific pitch, or has a specific pitch, then the heads are too tight. A bass drum which produces a specific pitch will conflict with the harmonic structure of your ensemble. On the other hand if the bass drum heads are too loose, the resultant tone will lack a full-bodied resonance and will be somewhat "soggy" in tone quality.

Bass drum heads, like all other percussion heads, must be balanced in order to produce the most resonant tone. Balancing the bass drum head would be done the same way as described for the timpani or snare drum head.

There are conflicting theories regarding the tension of the heads. Some say that the striking head should be tighter, and others say just the opposite. I feel that each head should have a different tension. In this way the vibrating head will respond with the striking head at a different rate of vibration and contribute to the indefinite pitch which is required. Therefore, each head should be of a different tension, but it can be a personal choice which head should be tighter.

The Cymbals

Photos courtesy of The Avedis Zildjian Company

Hand Cymbals   **Suspended Cymbal**
Picture 6–2.   Picture 6–3.

The better sounding cymbals are spun from a secret brass metal alloy. A good quality cymbal will produce many harmonics within its sound. The better the cymbal, the more harmonics it will produce. A cymbal should not produce a single predominant pitch. Cymbals come in a variety of diameters and weights and these varieties produce the difference in the response and pitch of the cymbal. Some cymbals respond quickly but have little sustaining power while others respond more slowly but will have much greater sustaining power. Generally speaking, the heavier the cymbal the slower the response, and the larger the cymbal the lower the sound. This is not always true, however, as all cymbals are hand-made and vary considerably in sound within each size and weight category.

Physical Characteristics of Cymbals

Selecting the Cymbal—The best way to purchase a cymbal is to know the type of sound or response you want, then go either to a dealer with a large selection of cymbals or directly to the manufacturer. Play a variety of sizes and weights until you find your preference.

I realize that this is ideal and not always feasible for many band directors. Therefore, I shall also give my recommendations for cymbal sizes although I cannot guarantee the sound you will obtain. For general playing purposes it is best to have a pair of 16" or 17" hand cymbals and a suspended cymbal of the same diameter. The hand cymbals should be either medium or medium-thin in thickness and the suspended cymbal should be medium-heavy weight. When finances permit, add a second pair of hand cymbals to complement the first pair. These should be much larger with a fuller sound to highlight those important cymbal solos in climactic places. These cymbals should be about 19" to 20" in diameter and in a medium weight.

Additional suspended cymbals should also be added when possible. Start by adding a larger and heavier cymbal of about a 21" to 24" diameter in a medium or medium-heavy weight. Although slow to respond, this cymbal should provide that extra power you might want in some cymbal rolls. It might be especially effective if played in combination with the other suspended cymbal. Next add a small, thin cymbal of about 12" to 14" in diameter for those quick, short cymbal "splashes." This cymbal should be very quick in response, but with little sustaining power or tonal depth.

The Cymbal Pads—On the hand cymbal it will be necessary to have some means of holding the cymbals. There are three styles of handles available for the hand cymbal. The first, and by far the best, is the rawhide strap and leather or plastic pad. This is best because it allows the cymbal to vibrate freely. Another type of holder is a rawhide strap with a lamb's-wool pad. Although the lamb's-wool pad is much more comfortable to hold it does reduce the amount of resonance from the cymbal by muting some of its vibrations. The third style of handle, which is totally unacceptable for any playing, is the wooden handle which is bolted to the cymbal. These handles not only limit the vibrations of the cymbal but they also cause undue strain on the cymbal crown and can easily cause the cymbal to crack.

The rawhide straps of the cymbal pad are held in place by means of a cymbal knot which is tied as shown in Picture 6-4.

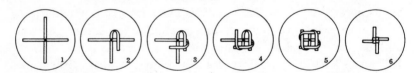

Photo courtesy of The Avedis Zildjian Company

Picture 6—4.   Cymbal Strap Square Knot

The Suspended Cymbal Stand—There are two common styles of suspended cymbal stands. The most popular is the single center-pole stand which has a shaft that inserts through the center hole in the cymbal. The cymbal is held in place by means of a wing nut and a rubber bumper. This is probably the best type of stand as it offers good stability for the cymbal and permits good control over it by reducing the amount of cymbal movement. These stands are adjustable in height and can accommodate various percussion set-ups which might require a variety of cymbals at different heights.

The other style of stand is an overhead one with a hook hanging from the top. The cymbal is hung from this hook by its hand strap. Its biggest advantage is that your hand cymbals can double as suspended cymbals, thus reducing the total number of cymbals you need. This is especially important where you have a limited budget. Any hand cymbal can be hung from this stand and then quickly taken off and used again as a hand cymbal. This type of stand does not provide as much stability when playing and the cymbal will tend to sway a bit more. This can result in some lack of control if care is not taken while playing.

This style of stand can be made at little expense from water pipe with a hook welded to the end.

Playing the Hand Cymbal

The Grip — The most important thing to remember when holding the cymbal is that the hand *does not* go through the strap loop. There is no need for the strap to have a loop. This is simply a result of the need for four ends on the other side of the cymbal with which to tie the knot.

To obtain the proper grip on the strap do the following: With the cymbal lying on a table, grasp the strap with the hand so that it is parallel to the floor and your knuckles are underneath the strap and against the pad. The thumb should also be placed against the pad. (See Picture 6-5.) Pick up the cymbal so that the thumb is on top and the knuckles are against the pad. (See Picture 6-6.)

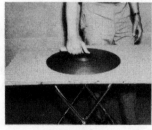 

Picture 6—5.   **Picture 6—6.**

The Stroke—When playing the hand cymbals hold the left hand stationary with the cymbal at about a 45 degree angle. The right-hand cymbal should do all the moving prior to impact. This method is preferred over moving both cymbals toward each other as there is less chance for a poor strike or a "vacuum" stroke. Strike the left cymbal at a *slight* angle so that the top edge of the right cymbal will strike the top of the left cymbal first. This angle must be practiced for if the angle is too great it may sound like a flam and if there is not enough angle a vacuum is likely to occur causing the cymbals to "lock" together and the sound to choke.

After the impact, the follow-through of the cymbals is important for the control of the sustained resonance. The right cymbal should follow through the arc it describes and end at eye level with the inside of the cymbal facing toward the audience. *After impact,* the left cymbal should also proceed to the same eye level position with its inside facing out toward the audience. The cymbals should face the audience as they are directional in sound and will project more clearly this way.

Damping—Hand cymbals should be damped if the part specifies damp, muffle, choke, a staccato note, or if the cymbal will continue to vibrate beyond the length of the note indicated. The cymbal is damped by pressing it into the body. This can be done by bringing the cymbal against the chest, stomach or arm pits, whichever is most convenient for the player.

Playing the Suspended Cymbal

The Mallet—The suspended cymbal may be struck with almost any type of stick or mallet. In many cases the music will indicate which type of stick is preferred. If not indicated, you must use your own judgment to determine the type of sound you think would be best. Most commonly, the suspended cymbal is struck with either a snare drum stick for single notes, or a yarn-wound marimba mallet for rolls. *Do not use timpani sticks on the suspended cymbal* as this wears them out quite quickly making them unsatisfactory for use on the timpani. Besides, the yarn-wound marimba mallet will produce a much better sound and response. When playing with two sticks on the suspended cymbal be sure to strike the cymbal on opposite sides of the center to prevent the cymbal from "tipping."

The Stroke—The suspended cymbal should be struck halfway between the center and the edge for the best tone. Occasionally a special effect may be desired and the part may call for playing on the "dome" which is the raised center portion of the cymbal.

The Roll—There are two methods of rolling on the suspended cymbal. When using snare drum sticks, or any other hard stick of this kind, it is best to use a bounce-stroke roll. When using yarn-wound mallets, or other types of soft mallets, the single stroke roll will give the best sound.

Cymbal Care

Cymbals quickly tarnish after use and they can never be restored to their original sheen. They can be cleaned, however, by using ordinary kitchen cleanser or copper cleaner. A metal polish can also be used if followed by buffing with a soft pad mounted on an electric drill or similar method. It is important that the cymbal be buffed when using polish in order to remove all traces of polish which could leave stains if not removed. It is also important that the buffing pads be soft as the temper of the metal, which controls the cymbal sound, will be destroyed if it should be heated too much while buffing.

On occasion a hand cymbal may turn inside out when struck. This is usually a result of either striking the cymbal at the wrong angle or with too strong a stroke. If you are having a continual problem with this your players are most likely over-playing your cymbals (i.e., trying to get too much volume or power out of cymbals that are too thin). The solution to this is to buy another pair of cymbals that are a heavier weight. Cymbals that turn inside out can be returned to their proper position by holding the edges of the cymbal in each hand and striking the inside of the dome against your knee. A cymbal which continues to turn inside out will weaken and eventually crack.

The Triangle

Photo courtesy of Ludwig Industries

Picture 6–7.

Physical Characteristics of the Triangle

Construction—The best sounding triangles are made from high-quality plated steel rod. Triangles are also made from other metal such as aluminum, but these are inferior in tonal quality. The tone of a good triangle will produce many overtones and triangles that produce one predominant pitch should be avoided. Triangles are commonly available in a variety of sizes ranging between six and ten inches.

The Triangle Beater—For the best sound the triangle should be struck with a metal beater. A variety in the sizes of triangle beaters is necessary to produce a variety of sounds and dynamics from the instrument. For soft playing, for instance, the use of a small beater will produce a soft sound while still enabling the performer to use a positive stroke. It is difficult to find different sizes of triangle beaters available commercially but they are easy to make. Buy some varying diameters of hard steel rod, which is available at larger hardware stores or building supply dealers, and cut into nine inch lengths. The more variety of diameters you have available, the more possibilities you will have for experimenting in sound.

Always purchase or make your triangle beaters in pairs so they will be usable in triangle rolls and two-beater playing.

The Triangle Holder—A holder for the triangle can be made from a wood spring clamp, similar to those of an outdoor music clamp, and a strand of nylon fish line. Drill two small holes in one side of the clamp about an inch apart and through these tie two separate loops of nylon line. These loops should be of different lengths as one will act to hold the triangle and the other serve as a safety line in case the first should break. The nylon loops should be short so that the triangle will not be able to "spin" while being played upon. Metal clamps can also be used and these are readily available from any hardware store and some percussion manufacturers. One problem with this type of clamp is that the sharp edges of the metal holes tend to cut the nylon line.

Do not use any rope, cord or line which is heavier than nylon fish line for the triangle. These tend to dampen the vibration of the triangle, thus reducing the tonal quality and the length of vibration. The use of wire should also be avoided since it will cause a distortion of the tone as the metal triangle vibrates against the metal wire.

How to Play the Triangle

The Grip—Hold the triangle in the left hand at about eye level for most playing situations. Holding at this level will help project the triangle sound over the ensemble. Do not play the triangle while it hangs from a music stand unless the part contains complex rhythmic patterns, a great number of rolls or there is not sufficient time in which to pick up the instrument. Form a "U" with your thumb and second finger and rest the clamp on top of the "U" with the open end of the clamp on the thumb. Place the index finger on top of the clamp. These three fingers hold the clamp firmly in place. The other two fingers are free to use for controlling the triangle sound. Turn the hand so that the triangle will be approximately parallel to the body.

Picture 6—8.　Holding the Triangle

The Stroke—The same basic stroke is used in playing the triangle as in playing any other percussion instrument. Hold the beater close to the triangle and strike with a quick "flick of the wrist" action, drawing the beater away from the triangle as if to draw the tone from the triangle. Use a stroke that is perpendicular to the triangle for maximum tone. Always strike with the tip of the beater near the top of the side opposite the open end of the triangle. (Place the triangle on the loop of the holder so that this side is on the right-hand side for right-handed players.)

When rhythmic patterns become too difficult to be executed with one beater the triangle should be hung and two matching beaters used. The triangle should be hung at chest level for optimum sound projection. When using two beaters play either on the outside of the triangle with one beater on either side of the top angle or on the inside at the bottom of the triangle.

Triangle Rolls—Rolls on the triangle can be played with either one or two beaters. When using one beater you should play inside the lower right-hand corner of the triangle alternating the beater between the two sides. For soft playing keep the beater close to the corner. Move farther from the corner for greater volume. When using two beaters use a single stroke roll and strike in the same areas as recommended above for general two beater playing.

Damping and Muffling—The triangle should be damped when short staccato notes are required or when you want to stop the sound from ringing beyond the length of the note. If the triangle holder is being held properly the last two fingers of the left hand are not involved in the grip of the holder and are within reach of the triangle. The tone is then damped by grasping the triangle between these fingers and the palm of the hand.

Muffling is used to produce a soft, veiled sound from the triangle. The resonance can be muffled by lightly touching the triangle with the last two fingers of the left hand.

Physical Characteristics of the Tambourine

Construction—The tambourine consists of a wood or metal

The Tambourine

Photo courtesy of Rogers Drums

Picture 6—9.

shell ranging from two to three inches in depth and seven to ten inches in diameter. Wood shell tambourines are easier to handle as they are lighter weight. A head, usually made of calfskin, is attached to one side of the shell. Some tambourines have tunable heads (usually made of plastic) which utilize tuning lugs similar to those on a banjo. There is not that great a need for the tunable head on the tambourine, as a calfskin head of such small diameter will not be affected greatly by the humidity and a plastic head will not be affected at all. Tambourines usually have either one or two rows of jingles mounted in pairs in the shell.

The Tambourine Sound—The primary sound of the tambourine is that of the jingles, not the head. The head should therefore be taught, as a loose head will produce more sound when played upon.

Tambourine shells are also sold which do not have any heads. These are good for sound variety and are especially useful on parts where the tambourine plays just a straight rhythm throughout. You can make a headless tambourine by saving an old tambourine with a broken head, removing the old head and sanding down any rough spots on the rim.

Recommended Needs—A well-equipped percussion section should have a small-diameter tambourine with one row of jingles, a larger diameter with two rows of jingles and a headless tambourine. With these three tambourines it will be possible to fill most any need. The more variety you have in sizes and jingles, the greater amount of sound experimentation your percussionists can make with the part.

Playing the Tambourine

The Grip—The tambourine should be held about chest level. It can be held in either hand although the left hand would be better for the right-handed player. Grasp the tambourine by the shell in the area where the jingles are missing. The thumb should rest against the head to dampen its sound and the other fingers are wrapped around the shell. The middle finger may be inserted through the hole which is found on most tambourines for a more secure grip.

The tambourine should be held at a 45 degree angle. If it is held in a horizontal position there will be a slight delay in the reaction of the jingles to the stroke and in very soft playing they might not sound at all. If the tambourine is held in a vertical position the jingles will continue to rattle after being struck, thus eliminating the crisp short sound which is desired. As one of the concerns of all percussionists should be avoiding extraneous noises, care should be taken that the jingles do not rattle when picking up the tambourine. When not in use the tambourine should be placed on a well padded table in the proper position so that it will not have to be turned over before playing.

The Stroke—The stroke used on the tambourine is the same basic percussion stroke. With the fingers set above the head, strike with a quick "flick of the wrist," then draw the fingers away from the head. Striking may be done with one finger, a group of fingers, the knuckles, the palm or the heel of the hand depending on the amount of volume and the quality of sound desired. Play near the rim to avoid as much head sound as possible. Strike on the head side right above the rim, on the head adjacent to the rim or on the underside directly on the rim.

The Roll—There are two styles of rolls that may be used on the tambourine: the hand roll and the thumb roll. The hand roll is executed by holding the tambourine as described above and rapidly rotating the wrist. When rolling in this manner a smooth continuous sound will result if the tambourine is held in a vertical position. The volume of this roll can be adjusted by the size of the arc described by the rotating hand.

The other style roll used on the tambourine is the thumb roll. This roll is especially useful for soft, exposed rolls, short rolls, or alternating single note and roll patterns. This roll is accomplished by sliding the thumb around the circumference of the tambourine head. Hold the tambourine at a 45 degree angle, start the thumb at the 5 o'clock position and slide in a counter-clockwise direction. Apply enough pressure so that the thumb sticks slightly causing the tambourine to vibrate. The dynamics of this roll can be controlled by the amount of pressure applied by the thumb. This type of roll cannot achieve as much volume or duration as a hand roll and therefore cannot always be substituted for the hand roll.

Most plastic and many calfskin heads will be too smooth to achieve a successful thumb roll. The embarrassment of starting a thumb roll which produces no sound can be avoided by gluing a piece of fine emery cloth to the circumference of the tambourine head. The strip should be about 1½" wide and go around the complete diameter of the head except where the hand holds the shell. This emery cloth provides a rough surface which reacts very well to the thumb pressure.

Special Playing Techniques—The volume of the tambourine can also be controlled by the height at which the tambourine is held. By keeping the tambourine below the waist it will sound much softer to the audience. If a crescendo is desired, slowly raise the tambourine to eye level.

When tambourine parts become so fast and complex that it is not possible to play with one hand, it is a poor idea to lay the tambourine on a table and play with timpani sticks even though this is commonly done. For fast playing which should be soft in volume, there are two ways you can play with much better sound and control of the instrument. First, rest one foot on a chair or stool and lay the tambourine on your leg above the knee with the head against the leg. The forearms can hold the tambourine in place by pressing against the rim near the body.

Both hands are now free to strike the opposite side of the rim allowing the possibility of much faster playing. The same two-handed technique can be applied by laying the tambourine on a thick, soft cloth. (A folded towel works well for this.) The thicker the cloth the better the tone. Lay the tambourine on its head and strike either on the shell or on the inside of the head.

If the fast part is supposed to be loud the above techniques will not work well as neither is capable of producing much volume. In that case you should employ the hand-knee technique. For this you place your foot on a chair or stool to raise the knee. The tambourine is then struck alternately by the hand and the knee. Hold the tambourine upside down so that the shell side is up. For loud playing you should play in the center of the head; this is the area which should strike the knee and which should be struck by either the knuckle or the fist. In playing in this manner, the knee is generally struck on the beat and after beat, and the hand fills in the rest of the rhythmic part. For example:

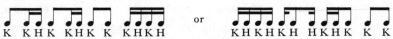

K KHK KHK K KHKH   or   KHKHKH HKHK K K

The Woodblock

Photo courtesy of Ludwig Industries

Picture 6—10.

Physical Characteristics of the Woodblock

Woodblocks are, literally, blocks of wood which have been

hollowed out to create a resonance chamber. The well-equipped percussion section should have at least two different size woodblocks for a variety of sound.

Playing the Woodblock

The woodblock may be struck with either a medium-hard or hard rubber xylophone mallet for the best tone; the butt end of a snare drum stick is used for a more woody sound. For a lighter, "clicking" effect, the bead end of the snare drum stick works well.

Strike the woodblock in the center with the same "flick of the wrist" described earlier. Striking near the open end may result in cracking the wood. For maximum resonance, hold the woodblock in the hand between the thumb and fingers leaving the resonance chamber exposed and keeping the palm of your hand away from the woodblock.

When playing parts that are too fast or difficult for one-handed playing, lay the woodblock on a padded table or better yet mount in a secure woodblock holder which is fastened to a *trap table*. (Caution: Be careful of mounting the holder on something like a bass drum rim as playing on the woodblock then produces an additional sound from the shell of the bass drum.)

The Tam Tam

Photo courtesy of The Avedis Zildjian Company

Picture 6–11.

Physical Characteristics of the Tam Tam

Construction—The tam tam is often referred to as a gong although this term is technically incorrect. (See gong, below.) The tam tam is hand hammered from a special metal blend which is kept secret by the manufacturers. The sound of the tam tam does not have a specific pitch but rather contains a large number of overtones enabling it to blend into any harmony.

Size—Sizes for tam tams vary so greatly that it would not be practical to list them here. A tam tam ranging from 26 to 30 inches in diameter is the best size for most needs.

The Beater—A heavy lamb's-wool covered beater that has a metal shaft and a weighted core is used on the tam tam. Avoid using ordinary bass drum beaters as they are not heavy enough to produce a full-bodied tone upon striking. Also have available a pair of smaller beaters for rolling. I suggest a pair of heavy, yarn-wound mallets for this purpose.

The Stand—The tam tam stand should be strong and well balanced as the tam tam is a heavy instrument and the momentum of the swing when struck can easily tip a poorly balanced stand. It should have large, rubber-tipped feet to prevent the stand from sliding or tipping when the tam tam is struck.

Playing the Tam Tam

The Stroke—As the tam tam is a directional instrument, it should be situated to face the audience. The player should stand to one side of the instrument. Because tam tams vary in their tone and responsiveness, the percussionist must experiment with the instrument to find the best area for striking. Generally this will be just slightly off center.

One of the characteristics of the tam tam sound is its slow response after being struck. In order to have the tam tam respond more quickly to the initial stroke the instrument may be "primed." To "prime" the tam tam tap it lightly before striking to start it vibrating. This tapping should be light enough so that the sound produced is not audible to the audience. With the instrument vibrating, the tonal response will be almost immediate upon striking.

Another idea, which Bobby Christian suggested in one of his clinic sessions, is to use a hard, yarn-wound marimba mallet. Place the mallet against the tam tam in the striking area and then strike *the mallet* with the tam tam beater. The hard surface against the tam tam acts to produce an immediate response. I have seen this demonstrated and it appears to work quite well.

The Roll—A single stroke roll is used on the tam tam. When rolling, use the yarn keyboard mallets described earlier and play with one mallet on either side of the tam tam rather than with both on the front of the instrument. This roll will create an easier playing position and prevent the tam tam from leaning to one side while rolling.

The Gong (Oriental Gong)

The Oriental gong is an instrument which has a specific pitch. This instrument should not be confused with the tam tam described above even though the tam tam is often referred to as a gong. (All Oriental gong parts are written for a specific pitch and unless this pitch is called for the part is probably for a tam tam.) The Oriental gong can be recognized by its flanged edge which is perpendicular to the face of the gong and by the raised "crown" in the center of the gong. Oriental gongs come tuned to each note of the scale and are available in a wide range of sizes and octaves. The gong is struck directly on the raised "crown" in the center of the face.

The Maracas

Photo courtesy of Ludwig Industries

Picture 6–12.

Physical Characteristics of the Maracas

Maracas are hollowed out gourds to which shot has been added and handles attached. These are to be preferred over the plastic or wood maracas. Avoid using maracas that are cracked as they lack resonance.

Playing the Maracas

The maracas should be held about chest level when playing so the sound will carry over that of the ensemble. Hold the maracas by the handles in a horizontal position with the index fingers resting on the top of the gourd. This places the hands in the same position used for the other percussion instruments, thus allowing the same wrist action when playing. Shake the maracas with the "flick of the wrist" action described. A gentle wrist action is needed for the clearest sound. By using too much wrist action the shot inside will move unevenly producing an indistinct sound.

When playing very softly, a clean, crisp rhythm can still be maintained. Hold the maracas in the same manner, but this time, instead of using the wrist action, move just the index fingers which are resting on top of the gourds and literally beat the rhythm with these two fingers.

Occasionally a part will call for a maraca roll. This is done by holding both maracas vertically and rotating in a fast circular motion. The vertical position should be with the handles down as it will then be possible to hold the maracas higher, thus projecting the sound outwards toward the audience more easily. This is important as not much volume is possible with a maraca roll.

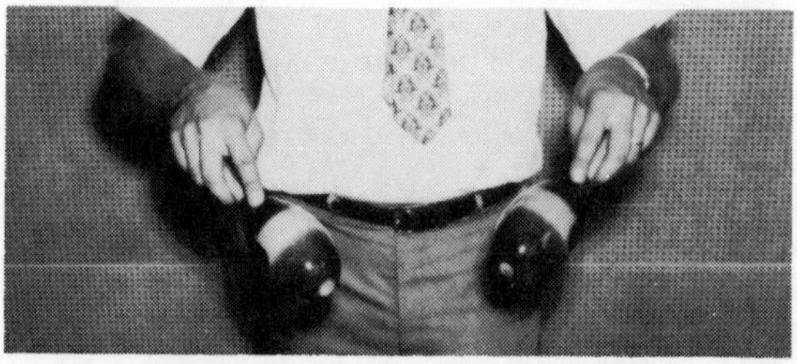

Picture 6–13.   Holding the Maracas

The Claves

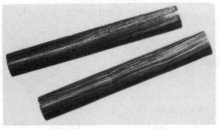

Photo courtesy of Ludwig Industries

Picture 6–14.

Plysical Characteristics of the Claves

Claves are usually made of rosewood and produce a high-pitched sound when struck together correctly. Within each pair, one clave should sound higher than the other. Claves that are cracked should be avoided as it is not possible for these to produce the clear-pitched sound desired.

Playing the Claves

The palm of the left hand should face up and hold one clave by resting it between the tips of the fingernails and the thumb and heel of the hand. Essential for a good clave sound is the space between the clave and the palm of the hand, which serves as a resonating chamber.

The other clave should be held lightly with the fingertips of the right hand. Holding this clave too firmly will cause a deadening of the sound. Strike the left-hand clave in the center to prevent it from shifting while being struck. Switch the claves from hand to hand and experiment with striking in order to find the highest, clearest pitch available.

Picture 6–15.   Holding the Claves

The Castanets

Photo courtesy of Ludwig Industries

Picture 6—16. Handle Castanets

Photo courtesy of Rogers Drums

Picture 6—17. Concert Castanets

Physical Characteristics of the Castanets

Authentic castanets are held in the hands and played with the fingers. This is a real art and one in which most percussionists are not skilled. Therefore, percussionists generally use either the handle castanets or the concert castanets (machine castanets).

Handle castanets are always mounted in pairs upon a paddle-like handle with either one or two pairs per handle. Each pair is mounted with one castanet on either side of the handle. Concert castanets are mounted alongside each other on a rosewood block. The well-equipped percussion section should have two sets of the single pair handle castanets and one pair on concert castanets.

Playing the Handle Castanets

It is best to use the handle castanets that have one pair of castanets attached. This style will be more precise and less likely to produce indistinct rhythms.

For normal playing, hold the castanets in each hand with the same grip that would be used for the other percussion instruments and move with a quick "flick of the wrist" action. For playing softly, hold one set of castanets in your hand and strike the handle just below the castanets with the fingers of the other hand. For fast, loud playing, place one foot on a chair or stool and, using both sets of castanets, strike these against the knee.

Playing the Concert Castanets

The concert castanets should be placed on a trap table and

are usually played with the fingers of each hand. A pair of soft, yarn-wound marimba mallets may be used for louder playing. The concert castanets offer a much more controlled and clear rhythmic sound than is possible with the handle castanets. Also, they have the ability to play complex rhythmic patterns with great clarity. However, they are not capable of producing as much volume as the handle castanets.

The Cowbell

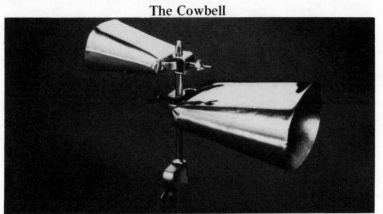

Photo courtesy of The Avedis Zildjian Company

Picture 6–18.

Physical Characteristics of the Cowbell

Cowbells come in a variety of sizes but the larger size is more desirable, for with a large ensemble it can produce a deeper and fuller tone. Cowbells are made of metal and are similar to the bells used on cows, with the exception that the clanger is removed.

Playing the Cowbell

Hold the cowbell in the left hand by the handle. The fingers of the left hand should rest lightly on the side of the cowbell to muffle the sound somewhat. It is important that the sound of the cowbell be muffled lightly for an unmuffled sound is too loud and will easily dominate the ensemble. If the cowbell is to be mounted on a holder, it should be muffled with a piece of cloth or cotton stuffed inside the bell. The cowbell may be struck with a variety of beaters or sticks and each will produce a different sound. Generally, the butt end of a snare drum stick or a rubber mallet will produce the best sound. Strike the cowbell either on the edge or the side. Personal taste and a little experimentation with sticks and striking will easily give you the sound that you desire.

The Guiro

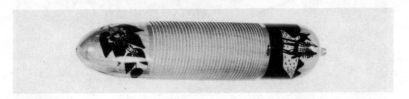

Photo courtesy of Ludwig Industries

Picture 6–19.

Physical Characteristics of the Guiro

The guiro is a large gourd which has been hollowed out and notched on one side. Many guiros are now made from wood but have the same characteristics as the gourd models. The wood guiros also have a pair of holes placed in the side opposite the notches to use as finger grips. A cracked guiro should not be used as it will not produce a desirable tone.

Playing the Guiro

The guiro is played with a small wooden stick which is scratched along the notched side of the instrument. Grip the guiro with the thumb and index finger of the left hand inserted into the holes in the instrument. Hold the guiro at a 45 degree angle and scratch with an up and down motion in the right hand. This scraping action should be fast to keep the notes short and the rhythm clear. A faster scratching action with more pressure applied will produce a louder sound which will aid in the projection of the instrument's sound. The tone color of the down stroke is different from the up stroke, so by using a combination of these two strokes a more interesting guiro part will result.

Bongos

Photo courtesy of Ludwig Industries

Picture 6—20.

Physical Characteristics of the Bongos

Bongos commonly come in pairs and have both a 6 and 8 inch diameter drum in the pair. They have wood shells with a head of plastic, calfskin or goatskin on one side only. Bongos are available with or without adjustable head tension. Only those with the adjustment should be considered for the school situation as the bongos must produce a sharp, high-pitched sound and the student should have a convenient means of adjusting the head to produce the correct sound.

Playing the Bongos

Holding the Bongos—The bongos may be held either between the knees or mounted on a stand. When holding between the knees the player sits on a chair or stool, keeps the feet together and grasps the bongos between the knees with the large drum to the right side. In the modern percussion section a player will often have to switch quickly from the bongos to another instrument, thus making it difficult for the player to get into the proper seated position for playing. For this reason, and the sake of convenience, many players prefer to mount their bongos on a specially made stand and play them from a standing position. Most bongos will mount on a stand by the use of a simple adapter. They may then be removed from the stand quite easily, thus making them adaptable to either method of holding. I recommend purchasing bongos which may be mounted on the stand to give this flexibility.

Striking the Bongos—From the seated position the bongos are almost always played with the fingers of each hand. Using the flat part of the first two fingers, strike the rim and the head of the bongo simultaneously with a "flick of the wrist" action. When the bongos are mounted on a stand the fingers are used in the same manner, but the bongos must be above waist level so that a good hand position is obtained for the wrist action. Mounted bongos may also be played with sticks to produce greater volume and a different sound concept. Timbales sticks, rubber mallets and the mallet handles all produce different but acceptable sounds from the bongos and all present possibilities for sound experimentation.

Timbales

Photo courtesy of Ludwig Industries

Picture 6–21.

Physical Characteristics of the Timbales

A set of timbales consists of two different size metal-shelled drums mounted on a stand. Like the bongos, the timbales use only one calfskin or plastic head on the top of the shell. The traditional timbales do not have counter-hoops but rather have tension rods which attach directly to the flesh hoop. This is important in order to achieve the proper timbale sound while playing because of the use of the rim.

Playing the Timbales

Timbales are played with special sticks that are made of hardwood dowels. These sticks are lighter in weight than the snare drum stick and consist of just a straight shaft. A light-weight snare drum stick or rubber mallet may also be used but neither of these will produce the true timbale sound. The sticks are held with the matched snare drum grip and the type of stroke employed is also the same.

The timbales are struck in three different ways:

1) In the center of the head
2) As a rim shot with the stick striking the head about halfway between the center and the edge
3) With the left hand and stick resting on the drum head, strike the rim of the drum with the left stick. When doing this the last three fingers of the left hand should extend out from the grip and rest on the drum head. The thumb and index finger will hold the stick in position.

The Conga Drum

Photo courtesy of Ludwig Industries

Picture 6—22.

Physical Characteristics of the Conga Drum

The conga drum, like the other Latin American drums, has one head on the top of the shell. The shell of the conga drum has traditionally been made of wood, is somewhat barrel shaped, and ranges in length from 22 to 30 inches. The head is usually made of heavy goatskin or calfskin and is held in place by tacks in the side of the shell. Some manufacturers have worked to improve upon the traditional conga drum construction by making the shell of fiberglass. The shape of the shell is sometimes altered to a tapered cylinder. Tunable conga drums are now available and they are to be preferred.

The tone of the conga drum is a resonant low-pitched sound and the player is able to produce two distinct pitches from the drum.

Playing the Conga Drum

Holding the Conga Drum—The conga drum is traditionally held by a sling over the shoulder. But, as described in the section on bongos, this is often inconvenient when switching instruments. Therefore, it is desirable if the conga drum can be attached to a stand. Conga drums also come in pairs to enable the player to get the two pitches needed, without employing the usual hand technique. This does make the playing of many parts much easier, but will also eliminate the true conga drum sound.

The conga drum may also be held in an upright position between the knees, in a manner similar to holding the bongos.

Striking the Conga Drum—The conga drum should be played with four fingers of each hand. These fingers strike as a single unit, with the left hand striking near the edge of the drum for a higher pitched sound and the right hand striking in the center of the head for a lower pitched sound.

The Cabaca

Physical Characteristics of the Cabaca

The cabaca is a large gourd which is covered by a loose

netting of beads. Some modern cabacas are made from wood but the sound and method of playing is much the same.

Playing the Cabaca

The cabaca is played by holding the netting of beads in a fixed position with the left hand while the right hand turns the gourd inside the beads to produce the sound.

The Tubo

Photo courtesy of Ludwig Industries

Picture 6—23.

Physical Characteristics of the Tubo

The tubo is a metal cylinder which is filled with shot and sealed at both ends. It produces a tone somewhat similar to the maracas but with a little more metallic quality and greater projection possibilities.

Playing the Tubo

The tubo is played by holding it with one hand at each end and shaking the instrument with a quick "flick" to produce a metallic clicking sound. Tubo rolls may be produced by moving the instrument in a circular motion.

The Ka-Me-So

Photo courtesy of Ludwig Industries

Picture 6—24.

Similar to the tubo except made with wood, the ka-me-so has a more subdued sound. The playing technique for the ka-me-so is the same as for the tubo.

Antique Cymbals

Photo courtesy of The Avedis Zildjian Company

Picture 6–25.

Physical Characteristics of the Antique Cymbals

Antique cymbals, also known as crotales, are made of bell bronze and are tuned to specific pitches. They should not be confused with finger cymbals (see below). Antique cymbals have a small hole in the center through which a short leather thong is inserted for holding.

Playing the Antique Cymbals

The antique cymbal part will specify the pitch which is required. Hold the cymbal by the leather thong and strike near the edge with a brass bell mallet. A plastic bell mallet may also be used, but the tone will suffer somewhat. Antique cymbals can also be played in pairs, sometimes with two cymbals at the same pitch and sometimes at two different pitches. When playing in pairs, strike the edges of the cymbals together.

The tone quality of the antique cymbals can be improved by adding a "vibrato." This is accomplished by rapidly shaking the cymbal(s) after striking.

If you do not have antique cymbals available, the orchestra bells can serve as an emergency substitute.

Finger Cymbals

Photo courtesy of The Avedis Zildjian Company

Picture 6–26.

Physical Characteristics of the Finger Cymbals

Unlike the antique cymbals, finger cymbals are made of brass and do not have a specific pitch. Unfortunately, some composers are confused as to the difference between the finger cymbals and the antique cymbals and occasionally will use the names interchangeably. The best check for this is to determine whether or not a specific pitch is required.

Playing the Finger Cymbals

The finer cymbals are played by wearing the pair of cymbals on one hand, with the thumb and index finger inserted through the elastic loop on each cymbal. They are then played by striking the cymbals together with a quick "flick" of the fingers. Finger cymbals may also be played in a manner similar to the antique cymbals by holding one cymbal and striking it with either a brass or plastic bell mallet. Because the quality of tone in the finger cymbal is not as refined as the antique cymbal, the tone quality is not reduced by using a plastic mallet.

A vibrato may also be accomplished on the finger cymbals in the same way as described for antique cymbals.

Temple Blocks

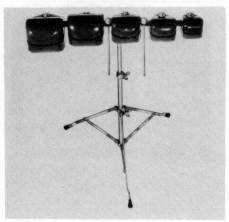

Photo courtesy of Ludwig Industries

Picture 6–27.

Physical Characteristics of the Temple Blocks

Temple blocks are hand carved from soft wood and are available in graduated sizes. They are most commonly used in sets of five. Each temple block has a definite pitch but they are not tuned to specific pitches.

The temple blocks are mounted on a stand for playing. The best way is to have all five blocks in a single row with the largest one on the left. Another method is to mount them in two rows with the three lowest pitches mounted left to right in the first row and the two higher pitches mounted behind and above these.

Playing the Temple Blocks

The temple blocks are played with soft or medium-hard rubber mallets. Snare drum sticks may also be used for special effects but should not be used regularly. Avoid using hard-rubber, plastic, brass or other hard mallets as they will damage the soft wood of the temple blocks. The temple blocks should be struck with the same stroke as used on all the other percussion instruments. For optimum tones strike on the top, directly over the resonating chamber.

Sleighbells

Photo courtesy of Ludwig Industries

Picture 6–28.

Sleighbells should be mounted on some type of board or handle and *not* played from a hanging leather strap. The reason for this is that there is little rhythmic control over sleighbells hanging on a strap. On the board or handle the player can control the ringing sound and will be able to produce a more definite rhythm while playing. One of the biggest problems in playing the sleighbells is the extraneous noises which result from picking up or setting down the bells. Great care must be taken in doing this and the use of a heavily padded trap table will be essential.

The Slapstick

Picture 6–29.

The slapstick is made from two pieces of flat wood one of which is hinged about two thirds of the way down from the end. Hold the slapstick so that the index finger is placed on top of the movable section of the instrument. When playing, strike the slapstick against the left palm while holding with the right hand. It is important that the index finger be placed in the proper position for, if not, the resulting slap will sound *after* the slapstick hits against the palm, causing a late attack. Some slapsticks come with handles mounted on both sides; these are played with two hands.

The Anvil

The anvil is not often called for in percussion music, so when needed it is hard to find. In most cases it is much easier to substitute for this instrument a steel brake drum. One can usually find these in auto salvage yards and with a little cleaning and painting they can serve as a respectable anvil. By a little experimenting the player can find the best place to strike the brake drum for the most resonant sound. I suggest using a hammer for striking. You might also try using a rawhide chime mallet if a great deal of volume is not required.

7

How to Teach the Drum Set Through Total Percussion

The Drum Set and Its Relationship to the Total Percussion

The concept of the drum set resulted from the development of the bass drum pedal around the beginning of the 20th century. With the advent of this pedal the need for a separate bass drummer in the pit bands was eliminated and one drummer could then play both the bass and snare drum. Hence the player became known as a "double drummer" who played the "double drums" or drum set. Over the years the techniques of playing this instrument have developed to the point where the "double drums" are no longer thought of in terms of one player playing two instruments, but rather as one complete instrument including the snare drum, bass drum, cymbals, hi-hat and tom toms.

For the student interested in playing the drum set, more is required than just good snare drum technique. Therefore, proper instruction from a qualified teacher is necessary just as it would be to teach a student clarinet or trumpet. Unfortunately, many drummers are self-taught, thus leaving some or all of the following techniques unlearned.

The most important skill which must be developed is that of ambidexterity. Even with the most basic beat, the drummer is required to play four different rhythms simultaneously with the hands and feet. The more advanced the part, the more complex these rhythms become. All drummers are expected to do more than just the basic beat patterns.

The ability to read music is another technique which is essential to playing the drum set, yet is often overlooked by students. They sometimes have the idea that the drummer just "fakes it" all the time. Nothing could be further from the truth, although I'm sure there are many amateur drummers around who do "fake it" when playing. All professional drummers have some type of music to read and guide them through the various arrangements. Although they are allowed a certain amount of freedom, they must be able to play the written part correctly at the times specified by the arranger. The drummer must be able to read and count all rhythmic patterns, but especially the more difficult syncopated patterns as these are more likely to be encountered when playing drum set parts. As drum set techniques continue to develop and drum set parts become increasingly more complex, the ability to read and understand rhythms is more necessary.

The development of good wrist and finger control at all dynamic levels is also essential when playing the drum set. This is required in order to maintain flexibility at any speed, a skill the drummer needs in order to maintain a steady beat.

Most of these skills can and should be developed through the study of the snare drum. Not until the student has a good understanding of basic snare drum techniques should he begin instruction on the drum set.

In teaching the total percussion in your school, instruction on the drum set must be included. First, many school music programs today are including stage bands. With this type of program, instruction on the drum set is essential to provide qualified players for your group. Don't rely upon the individual student to train himself to play with your group. Secondly, drum set techniques are becoming essential in concert band music. Wouldn't it be nice if each member of your percussion section were able to read and play such a part rather than your dividing the part between four or five players?

By teaching the basic drum set techniques to your students you will develop rhythmic independence and precision that can be utilized in all percussion playing. The students will develop more control of their playing and improve in their ability to maintain a steady tempo, a skill which is certainly essential to the percussionist.

It is virtually impossible to describe and develop good drum set techniques within the limits of this book. Ideally, the student should study with a competent percussion teacher, but I realize that in most cases this is not possible and that it will be the school band director who will have the job of instructing. In this chapter I shall present only the basic techniques of drum set playing in order to help the instructor begin the training of his students. Then, along with the use of a good method book (see Appendix), I advise the student spend as much time as possible listening to recordings of professional drummers to hear the styles and techniques used. Train your students to be observant when listening to these recordings. Have them listen to the drum and cymbal sound, imitate the rhythmic patterns and recognize the use of the basic patterns and how they are varied for interest. Listen to the drum part; does it blend into the total sound or does it dominate the group? Be sure the students listen to all styles of music and not just that in which they are interested. By listening to different styles the student will develop more ideas for playing. Also, a drummer rarely plays in the same style all the time.

Physical Characteristics of the Drum Set

Before beginning this section the reader should note that the information given regarding the basic drum set is only general. The sizes and number of instruments used can vary according to taste and the purpose they are to serve. The drum set as described here, however, will adequately serve the school for instructional purposes, stage band, pit orchestra and any other use that may be needed in the school situation.

The Bass Drum—The bass drum used in the drum set is

smaller in size than the concert band bass drum. It should range in diameter from 20 to 24 inches and should be about 14 inches deep. For school use it would be best to have a separate bass drum of the correct size for use with the drum set. A larger bass drum (marching drum size) can be used for practice purposes, but it will not produce a satisfactory sound for actual performance. The bass drum is usually muffled with a strip of cloth mounted on the inside of both heads. The desired sound of the bass drum should be a dull "thud." To mount this muffling cloth, remove the head from the drum shell and stretch a piece of cloth about 4 inches wide across the drum just slightly off center. (An old bed sheet can be cut to work quite well for this.) Have someone hold the cloth in place while you replace the head and counter-hoop. The head will hold the strip of cloth in place. Trim off excess cloth for a neat appearance with a razor blade being careful not to cut the head along the hoop.

The bass drum pedal should be equipped with either a hard felt or wood beater. The bass drum should be the lowest pitched drum in the drum set.

The Snare Drum—The type of sound desired from the drum-set snare drum is a full snare sound which need not have a great deal of carrying power but should blend well into a small ensemble and respond easily at soft volumes. In order to do this the snare drum should be smaller than that used in the concert band. This drum should be about 14 inches in diameter and the depth should be no more than 5 inches. The snares should be wound wire having from 18 to 20 strands. The metal snare drum produces the best sound for this type of playing, as well as for concert playing, and is used almost exclusively in drum sets today. The internal muffler in the snare drum will provide sufficient muffling for drum set use. For school use, any size snare drum can be used for practice purposes but a drum similar to the one described above is needed for performances. The snare drum should be the highest pitched drum in the drum set.

The Tom Toms—The basic drum set should have at least one tom tom, mounted on the bass drum. It is also common to have a floor tom tom of a larger size and/or an additional mounted tom tom. The mounted tom toms will usually be either 8 or 9 inches deep and 12 or 13 inches in diameter. The larger tom toms cannot be supported on the bass drum. These tom toms stand on the floor by means of attached legs and usually range from 14 to 18 inches in diameter and from 14 to 20 inches in depth. Tom toms are usually not muffled as a more resonant sound is desirable. If the drum tends to ring too much a strategically placed piece of moleskin can be used (see page 93). Tom toms should *not* be tuned to a specific pitch although they should each have a different pitch in order to provide a greater variety of sound. The tom tom should have two heads because this type will not produce specific pitches as will a tom tom with only one head. the sound of the tom toms should lie somewhere between that of the bass and snare drum.

The Cymbals—The ride cymbal is a larger cymbal in the drum set upon which the player will play various repeated rhythmic patterns. This cymbal usually has a diameter ranging from 18 to 24 inches. It must be chosen to produce a clear, precise sound without a great deal of resonance build-up, which tends to cover up the ride cymbal rhythm. A medium weight cymbal usually works best although you should try the cymbal before buying to be sure of the sound. The ride cymbal is usually the lowest pitched cymbal in the drum set.

The hi-hat cymbals are used in matching pairs on a hi-hat pedal. These cymbals usually range from 12 to 16 inches in diameter. The hi-hat pedal raises and lowers the top cymbal, clapping them together. Most cymbal manufacturers have cymbals designed especially for use on the hi-hat. These cymbals will produce a satisfactory sound.

The crash cymbal should be in a thin weight in order to produce a short resonance. Any diameter can be used depending on the individual taste of the player or director.

The Sticks—Thin, light-weight sticks are proper for use with the drum set. This size stick is appropriate for the smaller snare drum and will be consistent with the smaller ensemble with which it is associated. Wood sticks with nylon heads are particularly good for drum set use as they will produce a good sound when playing on the cymbal. The same size sticks should not be used in both concert and drum set playing.

The Drum Set Set-up—The set-up described here is for the right-handed player. The left-handed player may find it more comfortable to reverse the procedure. All instruments of the drum set should be located easily within reach of the player so that no stretching or difficult reaches are required while playing.

Photo courtesy of Ludwig Industries

Picture 7–1.   Drum Set

The bass drum is located directly in front of the player and is played with the right foot. The bass drum should have feet either mounted in the drum or attached to the rim. These feet will prevent the drum from rolling or sliding while being played. The snare drum is located slightly to the left of the base and closer to the player. It should be in an almost flat position about waist high when the player is seated. The hi-hat pedal is located to the left of the snare drum and is played with the left foot. The hi-hat cymbals should be about 2 to 3 inches higher than the snare drum and immediately adjacent to the snare drum head. This arrangement requires that the player straddle the snare drum stand with one foot on either side of the stand positioned on the hi-hat and bass drum pedals. The smaller tom toms are mounted on the bass drum and, if only one tom tom is used, should be located immediately in front of, and at the same level as, the snare drum. If two mounted tom toms are used, the second tom tom would be mounted to the right of the one described above. There are special mountings made to hold either one or two tom toms in this position. The tom tom should always be mounted at an angle, with the side closest the player lower, to eliminate the chance of the stick hitting against the rim while playing. If a floor tom tom is used, it is placed to the right of the bass drum immediately adjacent to the players right knee.

The ride cymbal should be located to the right of the single mounted tom tom and may be mounted on the bass drum. If two tom toms are used the ride cymbal is usually mounted on a floor stand and placed between the bass drum and floor tom tom. In either case the height of the ride cymbal would have to be slightly higher than the tom tom and angled toward the player to accommodate playing. The crash cymbal should be located to the left of the bass drum between the hi-hat and bass drum adjacent to the snare drum. This cymbal is mounted on a floor stand and should be higher than the snare drum. If there is a need for a cowbell or woodblock, these are mounted on the rim of the bass drum closest to the player. The player can also put a stick rack in this position to hold extra sticks and brushes as needed.

The player will find a stool which is adjustable in height to be most advantageous in enabling him to find the best position for his particular height. This is particularly necessary in the school situation where you will have students of different heights using the same drum set.

Basic Playing Techniques Used on the Drum Set

Basic Function—The drum set player has three basic functions which I have listed in the *order of importance:*

   1) To keep the beat

2) To create interest in the music through the use of fills, lead-ins and accentuating the high points or important rhythms of the arrangement
3) To provide solos when indicated.

Many young players reverse this order and think solo playing their main contribution. A good dependable drummer must, first and foremost, be able to maintain a steady beat upon which the rest of the ensemble can rely. In order to maintain that steady beat, the student needs to develop good coordination between his hands and feet. When instructing your students on the drum set be certain that they are able to maintain a steady beat while playing basic rhythmic patterns and have the needed coordination before introducing them to fills, lead-ins or solo material.

In addition to the basic functions listed above the player must also be familiar with all the styles of music he might encounter. This would include marches, polkas, waltzes, jazz and the many forms of Latin American and rock rhythms. Descriptions of the basic rhythms for all these styles can be found in good drum set instruction books (see Appendix). Another good source for learning the various styles of playing is listening to recordings of professional stage bands. I stress "professional" because I would question the authority of local rock group drummers, etc. regarding the various styles and techniques. Professionals need to know this information to qualify for employment.

The student will want to begin studying these rhythms as soon as he is at ease at the drum set, able to maintain a steady beat with the basic patterns and has developed a reasonable amount of coordination.

It would be well to mention at this time that either the traditional or the matched grip can be utilized when playing the drum set. As explained in Chapter 5, I prefer the matched grip for its consistency on all the percussion instruments. If the matched grip is used, the player will probably have to sit a little higher in relation to the drum set for optimum playing angle.

Basic Cymbal Rhythms—The basic ride cymbal rhythm used in 4/4 time is as follows:

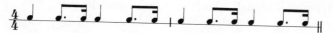

This rhythm might also be played to sound like this, although it is almost always written as in the first example:

The style and tempo of the piece would determine which version to use.

Another basic cymbal beat used quite regularly in the rock style is the repeated eighth note rhythm with accents on the 2nd and 4th beats as follows:

The student should practice these various rhythms until he has good control of them at various tempos. He should then add the bass drum, hi-hat and left-hand rhythms *one at a time* as will be described later in this chapter. Add only one additional instrument and practice that until the student has control of that particular combination.

Basic Foot Techniques—The feet control both the bass drum and the hi-hat pedal. In 4/4 time the bass drum, being the beat keeper of the drum set, will play either on every beat or on the first and third beats of each measure. These are usually good, solid beats as they must drive the ensemble along in fast tempos and maintain a steady beat in slower tempos. Generally, by playing on every beat the bass drum will tend to push the beat along more. Therefore, when a driving beat is required in faster selections, do not make the mistake of allowing the player to play on just the first and third beats for ease of playing. This technique is far better for slower 4/4 time selections.

While the bass drum is providing the beat of the piece, the hi-hat provides the after beat. In a basic 4/4 time pattern the hi-hat pedal will strike on the second and fourth beats of each measure. The hi-hat should be brought firmly together to produce a short, choked sound. There should be a minimum of ringing from the hi-hat cymbals either before or after the beat.

Basic Cymbal, Bass Drum and Hi-Hat Combinations— Combining the information given above, the basic 4/4 rhythm pattern for fast tempos would be as follows:

In a slower 4/4 time the basic rhythm pattern would be played as follows:

When playing in time signatures other than 4/4 time the same patterns are used—only varied slightly to accommodate the different beat. A basic 3/4 time pattern might be as follows:

The basic 5/4 time pattern might be as follows:

The cymbal rhythm described earlier need not be played on just the ride cymbal. For variety it can be played on the hi-hat while it closes on every second and fourth beat (standard hi-hat pedal rhythm). This causes the quarter note of the rhythm to ring freely and the dotted eighth and sixteenth notes to be short, choked sounds. The pattern can also be played on the hi-hat while it is loosely closed or tightly closed. All provide the same beat but with a variety of sound.

Left-hand Techniques—After the student has mastered the basic patterns and is able to play them steadily at various tempos the left-hand technique should be introduced. To begin with, the student should play only on the snare drum and after he feels more secure he might play these rhythms on any of the tom toms or combinations of drums as well. The left hand basically reinforces the after-beat rhythm established by the hi-hat pedal. The student should start by playing at the same time that the hi-hat does. Later this rhythm can be made more interesting through the addition of embellishments and other rhythms which fall on the second and fourth beats of the measure. Eventually, the right hand can stop playing the basic pattern and assist in the embellished rhythm on the after beat, but care should be taken that the student returns to the basic cymbal rhythm on the correct beat.

The left-hand beat for the basic rock rhythm also supports the after beats. This is necessary as the second and fourth beats in rock are so important. With the basic rock beat, the left hand would play as follows:

Embellishments of this style consist mainly of sixteeenth note rhythms.

Basic Brush Techniques—Brushes are used quite often and the basic beat is accompanied by the same hi-hat and bass drum beat.

The left hand holds one brush against the head at all times and slides it in a continuous clockwise circle. The circle is executed in such a way that the brush is at the 11 o'clock position on the first and third beats and the 5 o'clock position on the second and fourth beats. This action should produce a "swishing" sound. If a piece is written for brushes this sliding action is usually not written in the music but it is assumed that it will be played. The only rhythms written would be for the right hand.

The right hand is used to strike the drum and provide a beat. To start, the student should play straight quarter notes with the accompanying left-hand pattern. In order to do this the right hand must strike opposite the left hand. That means it must strike near the 5 o'clock position on the first and third beats and near the 11 o'clock position on the second and fourth beats. The student should practice this pattern until it comes naturally to him.

A basic brush pattern which is probably as common as the one described above is the same as the basic ride cymbal pattern. When using brushes, this cymbal beat cannot be heard as easily on the cymbal and the beat is often played on the snare drum instead. This rhythm is played along with the accompanying sliding left-hand technique. The placement of the beats is the same as when playing the straight quarter note rhythm described above. In addition the sixteenth note of the second and fourth beats will also be played at the 5 o'clock position.

Brush rhythms are played exclusively on the snare drum, for they do not produce as effective sound on the other instruments of the drum set.

Special Techniques—The three techniques I describe here are those which I mentioned earlier under the list of basic functions for the drummer. They are the fill, lead-in and solo.

1. *The Fill*—The fill is a rhythmic pattern usually two

measures long, which departs from the basic pattern. The fill can utilize any of the instruments of the drum set and serves to provide interest and add highlights to the piece. Because the fill will bring attention to the drummer and that spot in the music, its placement must be chosen very carefully. Fills generally fit best when interjected into the piece at phrase ends. For the beginner I recommend he develop and memorize a few fills which can then be used when needed. The student can then practice the fills and become familiar with their routine. Fills should be quite simple for the beginner, utilizing only quarter and eighth notes but stressing the use of the various instruments of the drum set. The bass drum can also be utilized as a part of the fill rhythm although at first it might be easier to maintain the same bass drum beat through the fill. The most difficult technique of playing fills is that of returning to the basic pattern without disturbing the beat of the piece.

2. *The Lead-in*—Similar to the fill, the lead-in will generally be from two to four beats long. The primary purpose of the lead-in is to highlight important entrances of other instruments in the ensemble or melodic high points. For instance, if the trumpets have an important melodic entrance, the lead-in would serve as a bridge from the previous part to the new. The lead-in might derive its rhythm from the rhythm of the on-coming part, if possible. Lead-ins, therefore, are used only at the beginning of new thematic, melodic or instrumental lines.

3. *The Solo*—The solo is essentially an extended fill. It can be as short as two measures but is more likely to be four, eight, sixteen, thirty-two or more measures long. The main difference between a solo and a fill is that a spot is provided in the music for the solo, it is not just interjected into the music at will. The beginner should start with short solos and practice them by playing two measures of the basic pattern, then a two measure solo, then back to the basic pattern. The length of the solo can gradually be increased. The skill which needs to be developed is that of maintaining a steady beat throughout the solo and then returning to the basic pattern without loosing the beat. Students should learn to experiment with solos both with the

rhythms used and the utilization of the instruments and sounds of the drum set. Much can be learned about playing solos by listening to good recordings which feature professional drummers. Again, I recommend that the inexperienced drummer work out a series of solos and have these memorized for use when needed. He will feel more secure this way than by trying to ad-lib as they occur. The more secure the player, the more steady his beat is likely to be.

Reading Arrangements—Most stock arrangements for the drum set do not actually indicate what is to be played. The student should look upon the drum part as more of a guide than as the actual notes to be played. The drummer must understand the style of music he is playing and what the basic pattern for that style is. Many times the part will only indicate the high points which need to be brought out or specific rhythmic patterns wanted. The drummer is expected to provide the basic beat, fills and lead-ins that are suitable for the particular style of the selection.

8

How to Train the Marching Percussion

The marching percussion will be the most visual phase of the program of teaching total percussion because most bands play to their largest audiences at parades and football games. Most schools start the fall season with marching activities and, therefore, the first appearance your band makes will be marching. A good marching band can be the foundation of a good year for the band. Dependable, well-trained percussionists in the marching band can add to the quality of the marching band. For this reason, the band director should be sure that his marching percussionists are performing correctly with proper attention to precision, showmanship and uniformity.

The basic function of the marching band is to provide entertainment consisting of music, pageantry and showmanship for parades, half-time shows, etc. As a part of the band, the marching percussion section shares this goal, which it helps accomplish by performing three basic functions. They are, to provide:

1) a steady, dependable and strong beat,
2) visual interest,
3) aural interest.

The most important of these three items is providing *a steady, dependable and strong beat* for the marching unit. Until your percussionists can do this, there is little need for visual or aural interest as your marching unit will not be able to maintain itself on the march. The secret of providing a good beat is to provide percussion parts suited to the ability level of the students involved. Regardless of how effective a particular cadence might sound, or a particular arrangement be with its 32 measure drum solo, if your percussion section is not able to play with a solid feeling for the beat and in a convincing manner, there is little value in using this material. The difficulty of a part does not necessarily make the percussion section sound good. Rather, it is the choice of drums used, the variety of simple basic rhythms and the exploitation of the sound colors available from the various marching percussion instruments.

The basic instruments needed for the marching percussion have usually been the field drum, tenor drum, bass drum and cymbals. There is a trend now to utilize tunable tom toms instead of the tenor drum and also to add marching timpani, timbales and bongos. If your percussion section is too small to field a reasonable marching percussion section, remember it is always possible to recruit other members of the band, especially if they play non-marching instruments, to play in the percussion. These people can usually be placed on cymbals, tenor drum or bass drum without much difficulty. However, this will require some modification in the type and difficulty of music and material you use.

Another important function of the marching percussion section is providing good *visual interest*. Careful attention to this can add greatly to the appearance of your marching unit and the general effectiveness of the visual aspect of its performance. The placement of your percussion on the field or in the parade formation contributes toward this. Place them for the best visual advantage, don't bury them behind other instruments, obscuring them from the audience.

When the time comes to purchase new or additional drums, the choice of color is most important for visual interest. The drums should be in a pearl finish, the brighter the better. Be careful, however, to consider how the color you choose will look with your band uniforms. It is most effective if the color of the drums can be in the school colors yet contrast to the uniform color. For instance, if you have school colors which are red and white and your uniform is basically red, a white pearl finish would be effective. Some drums are available in two tone finishes which might correspond to your school colors. It is also possible to mix the colors of your drums having some of them (tenor and bass drums for instance) in one color and the others in a contrasting color. Depending on your uniform and school color it might even be possible to choose another contrasting color which can be carried through in the marching unit with colored flags, etc. Before ordering any drums find a sample of the color you are interested in and check to avoid the possibility of having two different shades of the same color.

The important thing to remember is that you should not underestimate the importance of the color and finish of your marching drums as it definitely affects the visual effectiveness of your marching unit.

Also important for effective visual interest is uniformity. This, of course, is basic in all phases of marching and should also be employed in the percussion section. To begin with, all similar drums should be the same size and the entire section should have a definite color scheme.

All sticking should be uniform for all players of the same part and to accomplish this the drum parts and cadences should be written out with the sticking indicated so that each member will learn the part using the same sticking. Not only should the sticking be uniform, but the distance that the sticks are raised when played should also be the same. All sticks should be the same size and drums should all be worn at the same height.

One word of caution: don't expect to accomplish everything just described overnight. It will take a number of years to achieve these goals. In the first place you will probably have to use the drums the school already owns until they can, or need, to be replaced. Also, until you have a percussion section that can play the music and cadences with a good, solid beat, it would be premature to worry about uniform sticking.

The third function of the marching percussion is to provide *aural interest*. Part of providing a good marching percussion sound, again relies upon uniformity. All your field drums should be tensioned and tuned to sound the same. This also applies to your tenor and bass drums that are the same size. These parts should be played to sound like one instrument and this cannot be done if every drum has a different sound.

A variety of tone colors is also essential for aural interest. Make use of all the various tone colors available even if it might just be that of the field drum, tenor drum and bass drum. These three instruments can be used much more effectively by not having them all play at the same time. Write drum cadences which feature short one or two measure solos for each instrument to bring out its particular tone color. Additional tone colors can be gained through the use of cymbals, even two or three different size pairs, or you might use two or three different size bass drums to provide contrasting pitches. Also, the use of tunable tom toms, timbales and timpani not only provides tonal variety, but can also be tuned to specific pitches and incorporated into the harmonic structure of some of your arrangements.

The sound of the marching percussion must be short and dry, resembling a dull "thud," as opposed to the more resonant sound desired in concert use. The beat will be lost if there is an excessive amount of resonance coming from the drums. Also, the short, dry sound will tend to project much more, a quality that is desired for the band marching on a football field and spread out over 70 or 80 yards. All marching drums, therefore, need to be muffled in order to provide this good, clearly projected beat. Be sure to use the rudimental style of playing on the field drum. Tenor drums and bass drums may or may not employ the rudiments.

Physical Characteristics of the Marching Percussion

The Field Drum—Field drum construction is similar to that of the snare drum as described in Chapter 5. The main

Photo courtesy of Ludwig Industries

Picture 8–1.   Field Drum

difference is that the field drum is deeper and the snare should be made of either gut or nylon. Field drums are most commonly made of wood, until recently the only kind readily available. There are now some field drums made of metal. Either style of drum can produce an acceptable sound.

Field drums usually range in size from 10 x 14 to 12 x 16 inches. They should not be any smaller as they will then lack the projection power needed. Larger sizes will have difficulty producing a short, dry sound and will sound too low and similar to the tenor and bass drums.

The heads used on a field drum should be plastic and in a heavier weight than on the snare drum. Most drum head manufacturers have a specific head made for field drums. The snare head on the field drum should be a lighter weight than the batter head but heavier than the snare head used for the concert snare drum. Heads should be tight and muffled with a strip of cloth under the batter head only.

The sticks used for the field drum must be heavier in weight than those used for concert playing because the size of the drum is larger. If your players can handle them, 3S sticks have been a good traditional field drum stick. If this is too big for some smaller hands, use the largest stick suitable for the hand. Remember, that all your field drum players should then use the same size stick.

*The Tenor Drum—*The tenor drum should be constructed of the same material as your field drum, without snares, for a uniformity of sound within a section. Most percussion manufacturers make tenor drums, field drums and bass drums that are matched in construction.

Tenor drums are usually available in sizes ranging from 10 x 14 to 12 x 17 inches. Any of these sizes is acceptable providing it is a little larger than the field drum as its pitch should be between those of the field drum and bass drum. Many times the size of a drum will be determined by the size of the player who will have to carry the instrument. This is important as you don't want your players to grow weary carrying too large a drum. Remember, when marching, the percussionists are the only players who cannot stop playing from the time you start until you stop.

The heads used on the tenor drum should be plastic and, contrary to the field drum, both heads should be identical in weight. This is especially important if the tenor drum is to be carried in a vertical position and played on both heads. Some tenor drums are made with chrome bottoms. These also produce a good sound with the additional advantage of having good visual appeal. Do not use tenor drums that have only one head and an open bottom as these will produce a definite pitch, a quality not desirable for the tenor drum. (See tunable tom toms, this chapter.)

The sticks used on the tenor drum should be either wood or hard felt. I prefer the wood sticks as they are more consistent with the field drum sticks. Most of the wood sticks have rubber sleeves on the handles to improve the grip. The tenor drum is usually played with a matched grip because of stick construction, although if the drum is held by a conventional sling the rudimental grip would be better. In this case, you could use regular snare drum sticks on the tenor drum.

The Bass Drum—The marching bass drum is essentially the same as that used for concert playing except that it is smaller and should be well muffled. Marching bass drums range in diameter from 20 to 32 inches and in depth from 12 to 16 inches. Scotch bass drums are similar in diameter but range from 6 to 10 inches in depth. I recommend a smaller bass drum for it has the ability to produce a good, crisp sound and it is easier to carry. The smallest size I recommend is a 10 x 26 inch. Anything smaller than this will not project as well for the larger marching units. Do not use any drum larger than a 14 x 28. Even this size becomes rather large to handle unless you have a big player. In the school situation you can't always be sure of this as your personnel changes from year to year. I do not recommend using the extra large concert bass drum which requires extra players to help carry or pull in a cart. This bass drum cannot possibly produce a short, crisp sound regardless of how much it may be muffled. If you wish to use this large style bass drum for visual effect, fine, but don't rely upon it for your beat. Augment your section with one or two small marching size bass drums.

All bass drum heads should be plastic as these are not affected by the humidity, an important concern when you are playing out of doors. The bass drum head should have a medium tight tension to help reduce the resonance, but not so tight as to raise the pitch. Both heads should have the same tension and the pitch which results should be the same from both sides. This is necessary to accommodate playing the bass drum with two beaters. If more than one bass drum is used, the other drums should also be tuned to the same sound unless you are using different size drums for the purpose of having varied bass drum sounds within your percussion section. If this is the case, take care that the bass drums do not always play at the same time but alternate beats and notes within the part in order to achieve the full benefit of the various bass drum sounds.

The bass drum beaters should be either wood or very hard felt. I prefer wood beaters as they match the sound obtained from wood field and tenor drum beaters. The grip used would be the same matched grip.

The Cymbals—Marching cymbals are usually smaller and heavier in weight than those used for concert playing. The smaller size makes it easier to carry and play on the march and the heavier weight allows them to be played more forcefully without fear of having them turn inside out (see Cymbals, Chapter 6). Many cymbal manufacturers have designed special weight cymbals for use on the march.

The best cymbal pad to use is the plastic or leather. The lamb's-wool pad is also satisfactory although not as good a choice because it muffles the sound somewhat. The wooden handle, which is often promoted as a marching cymbal handle, should never be used under any circumstances. These handles not only reduce the resonance of the cymbal but also greatly increase the chance of cracking.

If you have enough players in your marching percussion section you might try using two different size pairs of cymbals. Having two different cymbal sounds will add dimension to your marching percussion. If you employ this technique, be sure to score the cymbals so that they are playing at different times so the different sounds are utilized to best advantage. If you have a player big enough to handle a large pair of cymbals these can be used effectively for the second or even third pair. Save these cymbals for use in climactic places in the arrangements you play.

The Tunable Drums—A rather recent addition to the marching percussion has been the use of tunable drums. There can be either tunable tom toms, timbales, bongos or timpani. All of these are tuned to a predetermined pitch, made possible because of having only one head.

When timbales are used, they are played in the manner described in Chapter 6. The bongos are usually used in conjunction with the timbales and are played with the timbale sticks. Usually a regular set of timbales (and bongos) is attached to a special carrying rack. These can be used quite effectively if your group plays a lot of Latin American numbers or utilizes Latin American rhythms for the drum cadence. If your group does not play in the Latin American style you will be better off using the tunable tom toms.

Tunable tom toms (sometimes called Timp Toms) usually consist of a set of two or three single-headed drums mounted horizontally on a special carrying rack. They are played with

Photo courtesy of Ludwig Industries

Picture 8–2. Tunable Tom Toms

either wood or hard felt sticks which should be held with the matched grip. Each drum has a distinct pitch which can add quite a different sound to your drum cadence and band arrangements. You can use up to three players on the tunable tom toms giving a possibility of eight or nine distinct sounds in addition to the field drums, a couple of different size bass drums, cymbals and possibly tenor drums. The tone color possibilities of a marching percussion section like this are far beyond those offered by just a field, tenor and bass drum.

Marching timpani are carried with one timpani to a player.

Picture 8—3. Marching Timpani

These are standard hand-crank timpani with fiberglass bowls to which a special mounting and leg rest have been added to aid in carrying. The marching timpani usually have a tuning gauge attached which can be used when tuning changes are needed on the field. They can be fairly accurate if plastic heads are used and the timpani is tuned carefully before the beginning of each performance. The marching timpani have retractable legs which enable them to be set down, if desired, during different segments of your band's performance. They may also be used in a concert situation when additional timpani are needed although their tone quality is not quite as good as the concert timpani. The marching timpani are available in 20, 23, 26 and 29 inch diameters. They can be an effective addition to your marching percussion if your section is large enough to use a couple of extra players. The marching timpani should be used sparingly and not within the drum cadence, although this is also possible. They are used primarily during the playing of the band arrangements. I would recommend the use of tunable tom toms before the marching timpani as they provide more flexibility and the greatest aural and visual interest for your percussion section and the entire marching unit.

Playing the Marching Percussion

The Rudiments—The rudimental approach is the only one the marching percussion section should use as it provides distinct rhythmic patterns, interesting accents and simplifies the problem of uniform sticking between all of the drummers. The rudimental style of playing must be used on the field drum and is an optional choice on the tenor drum and bass drum.

I shall explain the playing of three basic rudiments: the roll, flam and ruff. These three rudiments are the basis for all the other 23 rudiments and proper understanding of these can improve all the rudiments. A complete listing of all 26 rudiments can easily be found in many drum method books.

The rudimental roll—The rudimental roll is probably the most basic rudiment and one which every percussionist should know how to play. Although the rudimental roll is not used in most concert playing, it is an excellent means of developing hand coordination in the beginning student. For this purpose, the rudimental roll is often taught and played in a slow to fast style. Students who are beyond the beginner stage should practice the rudimental roll at a fast tempo for this is the way that they will most often have to play it.

To maintain a continuous sound on the drum the rudimental long roll is used. *This roll must retain a definite pulse of 32nd notes.* In this rudiment each stroke of the hand should produce two notes: the stroke and one rebound (bounce). This technique must be mastered before any other problems can be corrected. To play the roll as even 32nd notes, the hand action must be that of 16th notes. Thus for each hand action, two notes result and in essence double the time. To play the roll evenly have the student count 16th notes and use the stroke-rebound technique for each count. A well muffled drum with nylon or gut snares will help make the 32nd notes sound distinct.

The roll should sound even, and this is where many students fail in their playing. Following are factors which can cause the rudimental roll to sound uneven:

1) One hand stronger than the other
2) Grip not identical in each hand
3) One stick raised higher than the other
4) Sticks not striking in the same area of the drum head
5) Sticks not forming the same angle with the head at the time of impact
6) Stroke and rebound producing unequal volume in each hand
7) Stroke and rebound producing unequal rhythm in each hand
8) Sticks not moving perpendicularly to the head.

All the rudimental rolls should be played in the manner described above. This would include the five, seven, nine, ten, eleven, thirteen, fifteen and seventeen stroke rolls. In addition, these rolls also need to be practiced starting with either hand. The best way to do this is to alternate all rolls when playing them in succession (even the seven, ten, eleven, and fifteen stroke rolls). Also practice all rolls with an accent either at the beginning or the end of each roll. This is necessary as the accents in the music may occur either at the beginning or end of the roll.

The flam— The flam is a fundamental rudiment which is common to marching music and is an integral part of many of the other rudiments. The proper execution of this rudiment, therefore, is essential to most rudimental playing. When playing, remember that the flam should sound like one note which is stronger because two sticks are used to play. The grace note should strike immediately before the main note and together they make one sound. Avoid flams which sound like two notes or have both sticks striking at the same time. Other rudiments which utilize the flam are: the flam accent, flam paradiddle, flamacue, flam tap and flam paradiddle-diddle.

The ruff—The ruff is the other basic rudiment because, like the flam, it is an integral part of many other rudiments. The proper execution of this rudiment is essential to the rudimental style of playing. The ruff, in essence, is a three-stroke roll and should be thought of in these terms. By my previous definition of a roll the first two notes of the ruff are really played like 32nd notes and will occupy one fourth of a beat prior to the last, or main, note of the rudiment. Other rudiments utilizing the ruff are: the single drag, double drag, single ratamacue, double ratamacue, triple ratamacue, lesson 25, drag paradiddle no. 1 and drag paradiddle no. 2.

A student who is able to correctly play the roll, flam and ruff will have the basic skills needed for playing any of the rudiments. When teaching any of the rudiments be sure to analyze them in terms of these three basic rudiments. If this is done the rudiments should provide a good, clean rhythmic drive that is essential to the marching percussion section.

Carrying the Field and Tenor Drum—The field and tenor drum can be carried in a variety of positions when on the march. The most common is the use of the traditional sling (Picture 8-4). This sling passes over the right shoulder and hooks

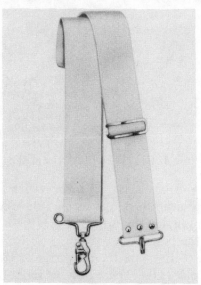

Photo courtesy of Rogers Drums

Picture 8—4.   Traditional Drum Sling

together above the left leg. When using this style of sling the drum should be waist high, both for ease of carrying and playing. Because this style of sling will carry the drum at a slight angle, the rudimental grip is the best choice to use with this sling. As the tenor drum will probably use a matched grip (because of the style of sticks), this is not the best method of carrying it.

When using a traditional sling a leg rest is also used. This leg rest fastens to the side of the drum and rests against the left leg to help hold it in place. Without this leg rest, the drum will probably swing from side to side causing difficulty in controlling the drum and the striking area for playing. This can also be the cause of many bruises on both legs. The leg rest should be placed between two tuning rods. Of these, the sling would then be attached to the left rod.

Another means of carrying either the tenor or field drum is to use the "hi-stepper" sling (Picture 8-5). This sling passes over

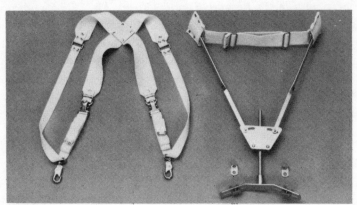

Photo courtesy of Ludwig Industries

Picture 8—5. "Hi-stepper" Drum Sling

both shoulders and has a special brace which rests against the waist to hold the drum high and away from the body. Because this type of sling holds the drums in a horizontal position the matched grip is the best to use.

The above two slings are the only regular slings that can be used with the field drum. There is, however, a third sling which can be used for the tenor drum. This is a vertical holding sling

(Verti-holder) which holds the tenor drum in a vertical position away from the body. This sling is similar to the "hi-stepper" sling mentioned above except that the brace is of a different design, to permit vertical carrying. When using this type of sling, the tenor drum is played like the bass drum, using both hands and a pair of matched beaters. When using this method, care must be taken that both heads of the tenor drum have equal tension in order to produce the same sound. I recommend this over the traditional sling for the tenor drum as it can easily adapt to the matched grip which is most common on the tenor drum.

Playing the Marching Cymbals—The marching cymbals should have the same type of plastic pad and leather strap as do your concert cymbals. The grip of these cymbals is different from that of the concert cymbals in that the hand passes through the leather strap and then grips the pad. This will result in the strap resting around the wrist while playing. In order to allow room for the hand to pass through the strap, it will have to be longer than on the concert cymbals. This strap acts more to prevent dropping than to hold the cymbals. When playing the cymbals on the march, they both move prior to the strike and not just one as in concert playing. One cymbal should be held high and the other low; bring them together at about chest height and alternate positions. Be sure that the cymbals still strike at a slight angle to prevent the "vacuum" stroke.

Cymbals can also be used as a hi-hat in certain numbers. When doing this, have the cymbal player hold the cymbals in a horizontal position while one of the field drummers plays upon them. The cymbal player can move the cymbals up and down in order to achieve the correct hi-hat sound.

Exaggerated motions on the cymbals can add much to the visual effect of your marching percussion section.

Playing the Marching Bass Drums—The technique used for playing the marching bass drum is somewhat different from that used in playing the concert bass drum. Because you are trying to obtain a dull, non-resonant tone from the marching bass drum it should be played exactly in the center of the head. It will also need to have both heads muffled in order to eliminate

all resonance from the sound. Muffle these with a strip of 4"
cloth stretched under each head to pass just slightly off center.
The drum may also be muffled by filling the drum one third full
of loose paper. Newspaper works well for this except that you
will be able to see the newsprint through the head. I find that
using paper table cloth works quite well as this is a soft,
absorbent paper and, being white, is not visible through the
heads.

Your bass drummer will find it much easier to play if he uses
a pair of matched beaters and plays on both heads. In using this
technique, it is also possible to write more complex and
interesting bass drum parts in your drum cadence.

The stroke used should be the same as for the concert
playing, i.e., perpendicular to the head with a strong wrist
action. Remember that the primary purpose of your bass drum
is to keep the beat for the entire marching ensemble. If your
band is spread out over an entire football field or a long city
block you will need a strong solid beat to unify your ensemble.

Playing the Tunable Tom Toms—As mentioned earlier, these
drums are carried on a special rack which will hold either two or
three drums. Each drum should be a different size, hence a
different pitch. When playing these instruments use the matched·
grip. Tunable tom toms can be mounted with stick racks to
enable the player to carry a variety of sticks with him. They are
usually played with wood or hard felt sticks but I have even
seen soft lamb's-wool beaters used for special effects.

The tunable tom toms are becoming increasingly more
popular with marching groups and in many cases are beginning
to replace the tenor drum as a part of the marching percussion.
The reason for this is that there are many more aural possibilities that can be achieved with three different pitched drums
than with one tenor drum. If you want to create an interesting
percussion section, both visually and aurally, I would suggest
using up to three players carrying tom toms of different sizes.
Have one player carry two big drums, another three middle-
sized drums and the third three small drums. In doing this you
will have available eight different-pitched drums that can be

tuned to form a full scale. Think of the possibilities this opens up for the drum cadence and various band arrangements. Using these drums alone you could create a cadence that would be unlike any with only field, tenor and bass drums. Add to this a couple of field drums, two or three different size bass drums, and two or three different size cymbals and you have the makings of a marching percussion section typical of today's sound in percussion.

The Drum Cadence—The drum cadence must provide a beat which the entire ensemble can easily follow. The parts should be rhythmically interesting but not so difficult or different that members of your marching unit have trouble finding the beat.

It is important that the director be able to write his own cadences for the marching percussion, for then he is able to construct a cadence suited to the ability of his players and can capitalize on the strong points of the section for that particular year. Also, as the instrumentation of the marching percussion is becoming so varied, it may be necessary to write your own cadence to best utilize the instrument you have.

For the young band which is not used to doing an extensive amount of marching, or the percussion section which is limited in ability, keep the cadence simple so that it can be played accurately and correctly. Nothing can destroy your attempts at marching as quickly as a percussion section that cannot play the cadence. If your percussion sections stops playing because the cadence is too difficult, there is nothing left to which the ensemble can march.

The cadence is usually 16 or 32 beats long and written in duple meter. There should be a definite ending to the cadence so that the ensemble can hear the repeat, or the beginning of a new cadence. The reason for this is to help them in anticipating the roll-off when signaled. If they don't know where the cadence ends, they can very easily be caught off guard at the beginning of the roll-off and might miss the point at which the instruments are to be brought up and possibly even the beginning of the song. Also, definite endings to the cadence help the percussionists in their memorization and in knowing where to play a roll-off. For most school situations, it would be best to have two cadences and play them alternately repeating each once before going to the next. This gives variety to the beat, yet simplifies the playing for the percussionists.

Be sure that the roll-off sound is different enough from the cadence so it can be easily recognized. The roll-off is usually 8 or 16 beats long.

For the percussion section with limited ability, an interesting cadence can be written without great technical demands by making use of the individual field, tenor and bass drum sounds, both independently and collectively. (See Example I.) Note the use of accents to add interest to the cadence. Also note that when one drum part is playing a more complex part the others are relatively simple. This both solidifies the beat for the players and serves to expose the rhythmically interesting parts.

Example I

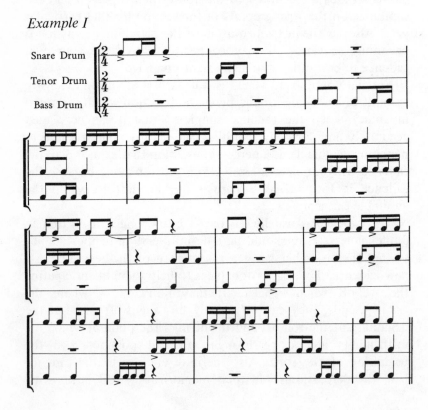

A roll-off such as in Example II would provide good contrast to the Example I cadence making it easily recognized by the other players in your ensemble. Be sure to designate some place

Example II

in the roll-off as the spot where all players bring up their instruments. Write the roll-off so this spot can be easily anticipated. In Example II the instruments should be brought up at the beginning of the fifth measure and this is easily anticipated because of the four beats of bass drum followed by four beats of solo snare drum.

For the section with more ability, the addition of rolls, flams and ruffs can make the same cadence even more interesting. The cadence in Example I, for instance, could sound like Example III, with the addition of embellishments.

Example III

The addition of cymbals to your percussion section should be used sparingly in the cadence. Do not use the cumbal as just a doubling of the bass drum part. (See Example IV.)

Example IV

Notice that in Example IV a more rudimental approach is used for the bass drum. Remember, the more interesting you can make each part, the better aural interest the section will have. Most of the old standard drum cadences rely too heavily upon the field drum with the bass and tenor drums providing only a beat in the background. This not only requires a strong performance by the field drummer but also produces a rather uninteresting sound from the marching percussion section. If the tenor and bass drum parts can be made aurally interesting, you will not have to rely solely upon the field drum part to support the cadence.

When utilizing the different sounds of the marching percussion section you might write a cadence as in Example V, using two different size bass drums. In this example, one player would play all the high notes and the other all the low notes of the bass drum part. As you can see, even though the bass drum ·part is beginning to sound more complex, it is really not difficult to play.

Example V

Example VI illustrates a roll-off which could be used in conjunction with the cadence in Example V to provide contrast and an easily anticipated point of instrument motion.

Example VI

When using tunable tom toms instead of tenor drums the sound possibilities become unlimited and, in many cases, without increasing the technical difficulties. (See Example VII.)

Example VII

9

How to Teach Musicianship Through Total Percussion

Musicianship is the one area which is most often overlooked by teachers in training percussionists. Having a good musical approach in playing any of the percussion instruments is just as important as developing good technical skills. Utilizing the total percussion program, besides teaching *all* the percussion instruments, you must also teach the student how to play each of these instruments in a musical manner.

The percussionist can and should be taught to play as musically as possible. He must be able to do more than play the right notes on the right instrument at the right time. Although accurate rhythmic interpretation and technical skill are essential to good playing, a musical application of these skills aimed at fitting the part into the total structure of the composition should be the true goal of the percussionist. Students must be made aware of the factors of musicianship: dynamics, phrasing, structure, form, style, tonal colors, balance and the relationship of all of these to their part. Musical playing will come about quite naturally if it is always expected of the student. Instruction in interpretation can begin with the very first lesson in the form of playing with the proper dynamics and accents. Instruction in phrasing and form is simplified when the student is studying the mallet percussion instruments, which should be taught simultaneously with the other percussion instruments. The student can then learn to relate this knowledge to the other percussion instruments as well. The areas of style, tonal color and balance can be taught through the ensemble and solo activities as will be explained later in the chapter.

The ability to hear the part prior to playing, and to understand how it is to fit into the composition, is essential to a musical performance. The player must then be more alert to what is happening in the composition and, in doing so, has taken an important step necessary in a musical performance, that of understanding the composition. A good way to develop this ability is to have the student practice singing his part. This can be done regardless of the instrument he is playing.

To summarize, therefore, musicianship is gained by refining the technical skills outlined earlier in this book and using these skills in a musical manner. The best way to accomplish this is to get the students deeply involved in playing the total percussion. This will take time for it requires a good attitude and mature understanding on the part of the students. In this chapter I shall present a few ways in which you can involve your percussionists more in playing the total percussion musically.

Playing the Percussion Part in a Musical Manner

When playing the percussion part of a full band arrangement the percussionist can benefit by listening carefully to the other instruments. The percussion part must agree stylistically with the rest of the band or else it will detract from the performance. As some of the following examples will show, the written part does not always provide sufficient information to allow an accurate performance. This is where the percussionist's ability for stylistic interpretation plays an important part in his playing. This skill should also be taught as a regular part of the percussionist's musical training.

Stylistic Interpretation—One example of interpreting a part can be illustrated by taking a bass drum part and placing it into two different styles of music. In so doing, this part cannot be played the same, even though the notes might be the same. For this example let us use a simple repeated quarter note pattern:

If this were a part from a march it should be played to sound like this:

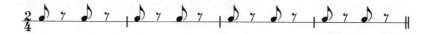

As explained in Chapter 6, this is accomplished by muffling the left head with the hand, the right head with the knee and playing directly in the center of the head for a minimum of resonance. If this same part were from a slower, more legato piece, it should be played to sound like this:

To do this you should not muffle the drum at all and should play in the usual striking area. The point is that a part cannot be played in the same manner when written in two different styles of music.

Another problem of interpretation can be illustrated with the following bass drum example:

Playing this part at a moderately fast tempo most players would strike the bass drum on the proper beat and consider it played correctly. This is not correct, however, for if the composer had wanted all the notes to sound the same length, he would have written the part like this:

Most likely, in an example like this, the half, quarter and staccato quarter notes have been utilized to correspond to a rhythm the band is playing. If your player merely strikes the drum on the proper beat he is essentially ignoring the true rhythm of the part. Controlling the length of the note on the bass drum involves using the hand and knee to muffle the amount of resonance. In this example, the player might muffle lightly with the left hand when playing the quarter notes. On the half notes he could remove his left hand completely and return it at the end of the half note duration. The staccato quarter notes could be played with both the left hand and right knee against the heads to remove all resonance. The interpretation problem here is that the percussionist must read and *play* all rhythms accurately and this includes controlling the *length* of the notes when possible.

Another problem in interpretation is typified by the following. You may encounter a triangle part which looks like this:

By examining the other band parts, however, you might find that some of the other instruments are playing this rhythm at the same time:

In this case the composer has not given the percussionist enough information about the part to allow him to play it correctly. The triangle has a relatively long resonance and without any muffling between notes this part would sound like a continuous note with accents on each beat. By listening to the band it becomes clear how the triangle part is to be played. It can be done quite easily with the use of the fingers for muffling as described in Chapter 6.

It is necessary to be aware of what the band is playing in order to play the percussion part correctly. The percussionist must learn to listen to the other band parts and correlate his part to that. This would also include balancing the volume of the percussion part to that of the rest of the band.

Rhythmic Interpretation—Besides interpreting the part stylistically the player must also interpret the part rhythmically in terms of natural, unnatural and agogic (implied) accents to help clarify the part and play in a musical manner.

The natural accents are those which create the pulse of the meter. We are all aware of these accents but often do not think to teach our percussionists to play them. A part similar to the following should be played with the accents indicated even though they probably would not be written out:

If this is not done, the meter of a piece can easily be destroyed by the percussion. For example, the following rhythm, if played without any accents, would leave the listener without any feeling of meter:

By using the natural accents, however, the part can be clarified to the listener:

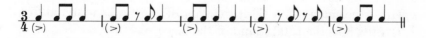

Unnatural accents are those which are played off the beat of the regular pulse. Syncopated rhythms present a good example of this. The example below, would probably be written without any accents but should be played as indicated utilizing both the natural and unnatural accents:

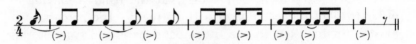

Sometimes composers will utilize agogic accents by writing longer note values. In the example below, the part would be played with the accents indicated even though they would not be written:

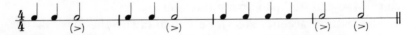

An exception to this would be if the other band parts had a different accent pattern indicated. The percussionist must then observe this in order to play in stylistic agreement with the band.

Tonal Colors Affect Musicianship—The percussionist can make his performance more musical by experimenting to find the best tone colors available for the particular part he is playing. By stressing this experimentation *in the rehearsal period* you will encourage your percussionist to think about the musical implication of the part. The most obvious example of this can be found in a typical suspended cymbal part. Quite often the part will simply be marked as suspended cymbal, or cymbal with stick. Here's where the initiative and experimentation of the percussionist can take over. Don't be content to have him hit the cymbal with any stick that is handy. Obviously there are many sticks that could be used on the cymbal and from these you can achieve a multitude of sounds. What did the composer have in mind? Nobody knows if it isn't marked, but with experimentation the percussionist can find the sound that best fits into the total sound of the piece.

Almost all the percussion instruments are capable of producing a variety of tonal colors. This variation is controlled mostly by the striking object and the striking area. The percussionist should know the possibilities and be able to control these sounds at will. Much of this is explained more fully in the preceding chapters. The point is that the percussionist should not just hit the instrument when he plays, but should be thinking about the sound which will result and whether it will fit musically into the composition. By listening carefully to his part, coupled with understanding tonal colors, he can give a musical performance on any of the percussion instruments.

To summarize, a musical performance of percussion parts can result by observing the following:

1) Adjust the parts to the style and tempo of the music
2) Play all note lengths correctly, if possible to control
3) Listen, and conform, to the other instrumental parts in the band arrangement
4) Pay careful attention to the use of natural, unnatural and implied accents, not all of which are usually marked
5) Experiment with, and gain control of, the various tonal colors available from each percussion instrument.

There is one last item I would like to mention regarding the musical performance of a percussion part. Occasionally, especially in easier music, a composer will write a drum part just to keep the percussionists busy. These compositions are fairly obvious because the part is usually simple, unmusical and completely out of place. It is virtually impossible to perform a part like this musically because it was not conceived musically. If you encounter such a part, don't hesitate to edit it; either take it out completely, or alter the instrumentation so that it can be done more musically.

The Percussion Ensemble as an Aid to Teaching Musicianship

The percussion ensemble is a form of small group instruction that can provide your percussionists with the means of improving musicianship, developing technique and creating an understanding of playing the total percussion. Through the ensemble, the student will have a chance to play a greater variety of percussion instruments, learn more about specific technical skills required for each, and learn how to play them in a musical manner.

Developing Musical Skills—The percussion ensemble experience is quite unlike that of playing percussion parts in a band arrangement. Of course, the same skills and knowledge are required but there is the additional challenge of achieving a musical performance without the benefit of relating to the phrasing and interpretation of the band. Each player must perform musically if the ensemble is to sound musical. This means that careful attention must still be given to those qualities of musicianship described above, but in addition the players must become aware of another quality, that of balancing their parts with each other.

The percussion ensemble offers an excellent opportunity to develop the skill of balancing. When playing percussion ensemble music, the instructor and student must remember that certain instruments have more projection power than others and that these instruments will tend to dominate. Generally, the larger the instrument the more projection power it will have. In addition, the snare drum and cymbals can easily be too loud in the ensemble if not played with a conscious effort to control the volume. The mallet instruments will generally not project as well. Students must always be alert to volume and adjust to create a balanced sound. Volume markings, therefore, can only be relative guidelines for each player, and the actual volume played can only be determined by the particular instruments involved at that time.

A factor which will help balance the instruments is their placement within the percussion ensemble. As a general rule, always place the instruments with the greatest projection power near the back. Of course, this is not always possible as many times a student will play more than one instrument and will not be able to change positions.

When playing in the band, the placement of the instruments within the section will not have as much effect on the volume as in the ensemble. However, the students should have developed an awareness of the projection capabilities of the various percussion instruments and, keeping this in mind while playing, can better balance percussion parts with the rest of the band.

In developing the musicianship of your percussion students a good yearly, or semester, project would be to have each student compose a short piece for percussion. By writing for the percussion ensemble you have the perfect vehicle needed for performing and discussing the problems which occurred in the composition. By encouraging your percussion students to write music you will further stimulate their thinking along the lines of a musical performance. In composing they will need to utilize the information they have learned about the various tone colors, rhythmic and stylistic interpretation, projection powers, technical difficulties and notational problems, thus aiding the learning process. All of this will make them even more aware of the musical approach needed for the percussion.

Improving Technical Skills—The percussion ensemble can serve as a training group to strengthen the weaker performing areas of all your percussionists. If you are just beginning a program of teaching total percussion it is likely your players are going to be more advanced on certain instruments and weaker or totally inexperienced on others. Through careful selection of the ensemble music, and the assignment of parts, you can utilize this group to train your players on their weaker instruments. This gives them a chance to learn the techniques required to play the instruments before being expected to do so in the band.

A distinct advantage to using the percussion ensemble, instead of the band, for training your percussionists is that the difficulty of the music can be controlled to *their* ability level. In the band situation, the whole band needs to be considered in deciding how difficult the music should be. Oftentimes if a piece has a challenging percussion part, it may either be too easy or too hard for the rest of the band.

Improving the Image of Percussion—The percussion ensemble can also serve to show others the complexities and challenges offered the percussion player. Understanding that the percussion can and must be played in a musical manner will provide a better image of the percussionist to his peers. This image can be developed in two ways: first, through performances by the percussion ensemble, coupled with explanations and demonstrations of the various instruments being used, and secondly, by recruiting non-percussion players to fill in on the less demanding parts when you have a number which requires many players. This gives the non-percussion players both the chance to play some percussion instruments (a secret desire for many instrumentalists in high school) and to strengthen their musical growth by forcing them to think musically without the aid of a melodic instrument.

Because of the experiences that the percussion ensemble can offer, I suggest that all percussion students participate in the ensemble. The benefits both to the students and the band will make any effort toward this goal worthwhile. The understanding, skill and musicianship which the student develops through this experience will eventually transfer to his playing in the band.

The percussion ensemble should be thought of in terms of being supplemental instruction and should not substitute for any form of instruction that is presently in existence. The rehearsal for the ensemble should not replace individual or group lessons nor should it replace sectionals or take time from the full band rehearsals. This, seemingly, does not allow much time for ensemble practice. In my own experience I have found that a weekly evening rehearsal works quite nicely. This may or may not be possible in your situation. You might also be able to schedule a rehearsal during the noon hour or a school activity period.

Solos and Ensembles as a Means of Developing Musicianship

In addition to the band and percussion ensemble experience,

each student should be given the opportunity to do some study of solo material. If you are undertaking a serious program of teaching the total percussion it will be most beneficial to concentrate in the area of multiple percussion solos. Here the student is faced with the problem of performing musically on a variety of percussion instruments, without any conductor or other students to help toward the musical effect. Also, the multiple percussion solo will present the student with the additional problems of playing a variety of instruments at one time, developing good tone control and instrument placement. Multiple percussion solos will often introduce the students to new ideas on how to play the percussion instruments. It will encourage them to experiment in percussion sounds and will expose them to a greater number of possible sounds. Although there are multiple percussion parts in some percussion ensemble and band arrangements, the student is not often going to experience this form of playing. The multiple percussion solo, therefore, is a necessary part of the total percussion training. Because it can be such a good source of both technical and musical training, I suggest that the multiple percussion solo be used regularly from the beginning of the student's training.

It is also important to supplement the multiple percussion study with solos on the individual percussion instruments. All students should come in contact with snare drum, timpani and mallet percussion solos. This will give them a chance to develop their musical and technical skills on the individual instruments to a greater degree than ever possible in multiple percussion solos. With this type of solo the student can work on the fine details of playing a particular percussion instrument.

If possible, you should have the student study at least two solos per year. In many states there are solo festivals held each year. These can provide a good incentive for the students toward solo study. If this is not available the student should still study the solos as a part of the lesson plan even though there may not be any performance possibilities available.

For the three of four years you have this student under your care I suggest a plan similar to the following for the study of solo material:

1st year– 1 multiple percussion solo
            1 snare drum solo
2nd year–1 multiple percussion solo
            1 timpani solo
3rd year– 1 multiple percussion solo
            1 mallet percussion solo
4th year– 1 multiple percussion solo
            1 solo of the student's choice

In addition to the solo experience, don't forget the value in encouraging your students to participate in small ensembles. With a background in the total percussion, musical performance, and the experience with the percussion ensemble, your students will be able to do a lot of these small ensembles almost completely by themselves. One very beneficial experience in the duet area, which will challenge the students' musical ability, is the performance of mixed duets (i.e., duets involving one percussion and one other instrument besides piano). This also presents a challenge and good experience to the non-percussion player.

Summary–It can be concluded that musicianship must be taught to the percussion student and this instruction must be a part of every lesson. Musicianship becomes easier to teach the more involved your students become in playing the total percussion. All percussion students should have the experience of solo and ensemble playing to fully develop their musical and technical skills on all of the percussion instruments and this can be done most effectively through the use of the multiple percussion solo and the percussion ensemble.

10

How to Organize
the Successful
Percussion Section

Utilizing the Percussion Personnel

Choose a Section Leader—In organizing and running a successful total percussion section there are many small details that must be taken care of. The appointment of a section leader can serve to relieve the director of these details, thus giving him more time to devote to his teaching.

The section leader should be chosen on the basis of dependability, maturity, leadership, and ability in the total percussion. In performing his duties he will assume responsibility for the entire section and must maintain authority within the section. If you are just beginning a program of teaching the total percussion you may not yet have a student with ability in the total percussion. In that case choose the most mature and dependable individual in the section. Listed below are the responsibilities that should be assumed by your section leader:

1) Assign the parts to the other members of the section. When a piece of music is passed out, the section leader should

be given the percussion parts in advance. It is his responsibility to look over the parts and determine the number of players needed, the difficulty of each part and who is able to play it. (See more about the assignment of the parts in the discussion below.)

2) Make a note of any instrument needed that is not available and inform the director of this immediately. The director will then have to obtain the instrument, substitute for it, or, if the instrument is vital to the piece and not obtainable, perhaps even decide not to play the music. The director can help the section leader if he gives him the percussion parts in advance. This will allow time to obtain needed instruments before the other parts are passed out.

3) Indicate to the director if there will not be enough players available in the section to play all the parts. This should be done immediately after receiving the parts (which have been passed out in advance). The director can then decide if he should recruit other players from the band for that number, leave out some of the parts or perhaps not play the piece.

4) Keep the director alert to any instruments which are broken or damaged and in need of repair or replacement. All instruments should be checked regularly, not just those that are needed for a particular day. The section leader can either be in charge or assist in the monthly and yearly maintenance program described later in this chapter. The section leader should also inform the director of any damage which he knows has been caused through careless or abusive handling either by percussion students or other band members. The percussion instruments hold a great attraction for most students, which can easily lead to reckless handling. By having a student responsible for their condition you can reduce this type of damage.

Because the section leader's responsibilities are quite involved, they cannot be passed from student to student very easily. If so, you will spend much of the time you were to have gained instructing each new section leader and helping him with his duties and responsibilities. I suggest instead that you carefully select one student to serve as section leader for the entire year.

Assigning the Percussion Parts—Under the total percussion program, the percussion parts should be assigned so that all percussion students will receive equal opportunities in playing all of the percussion instruments. Of course, parts must be assigned to students who can play them, as the band rehearsal is not the place for a student to try playing any instrument for the first time. If you are teaching the total percussion in lessons, however, all of your students will have different degrees of experience on each instrument. Some parts require more advanced technical skills than others. It is possible, therefore, to assign students to each instrument and still have it within their ability.

The assignment of parts must also be based on a rotational system. This will enable each student to play on each instrument an equal amount of times. This also prevents the same student from being left out if all the section members are not needed. The section leader must keep a record of the assignments made for music already passed out and those made earlier in the year.

When assigning parts on a rotational basis, you do create more movement and instrument changes between the numbers on your concert. This can be done fairly easily, however, as students get used to the numbers and instruments needed. You can help them, in fact, by determining the order of the program well in advance and by following this order occasionally in rehearsal. If you have a number which requires a lot of percussion equipment, either schedule it at the beginning of the program or after an intermission to allow sufficient time for setting up.

Example One shows a poor, unbalanced assignment chart, for the parts are assigned to the player who is strongest in each area. Jim is the best timpani player, Cathy plays all the mallet parts, Sue is the best snare drum player, and Bill and Bob aren't as skilled and are assigned all the accessory percussion instruments. Assignments of this kind do not contribute toward building a total percussion program. How are Bill and Bob ever going to learn how to play the snare drum, timpani or mallet instruments? Don't you think that Bill might become a problem

Example One

Percussion Assignments for Winter Concert

	Piece "A"	Piece "B"	Piece "C"	Piece "D"	Piece "E"
Jim	Timp	Snare Drum	Timp	Timp	Timp
Cathy	Bells		Bells & Xylophone	Bells & Vibes	Cowbell
Sue	Snare Drum		Snare Drum	Snare Drum	Timbales
Bill	Bass Drum	Bass Drum	B.D. & Woodblock	Bass Drum	Claves
Bob	Cymbal	Cymbal	Sus. Cym. & Triangle		Maracas

Example Two

Percussion Assignments for Winter Concert

	Piece "A"	Piece "B"	Piece "C"	Piece "D"	Piece "E"
Jim	Timp	Snare Drum	Bells & Triangle	Bass Drum	Maracas
Cathy	Bass Drum	Cymbal	Snare Drum		Cowbell
Sue	Bells		Sus. Cym. & Xylophone	Snare Drum	Timp
Bill	Snare Drum	Bass Drum	Timp	Bells & Vibes	Claves
Bob	Cymbal		B.D. & Woodblock	Timp	Timbales

student if all he ever plays is bass drum? Wouldn't you become bored after awhile and begin to "fool around" to make things more "interesting" during the rehearsal? What about your better players—Jim, Cathy and Sue? They too should have the opportunity of playing all the percussion instruments. If each of these students is specializing on one percussion instrument you are teaching against the total percussion approach. There is no value in just teaching the total percussion in lessons, it must be utilized under performance situations.

Example Two shows a much better balanced assignment of the same parts. Although the example is fictitious, the thought behind these assignments might have been as follows. (This is the type of thinking that you and your section leader must do in order to implement your total percussion program into the band performance.)

"In Piece 'A' the timpani part is quite difficult, so keep Jim on that part. The snare drum is not hard and it will give Bill a chance to play the snare drum in concert. The bell part is only moderately hard, and because Sue has been improving on the bells this will give her a nice challenge. In piece 'B' only three players are needed. Because Jim, Bill and Cathy didn't play in one song on the last concert the parts can be assigned to them this time. In piece 'C' the timpani part is easy and will give Bill a chance to play the timpani. The snare drum part is moderately hard but well within the ability of Cathy. Bob can play the bass drum and woodblock. They are not difficult parts but there is a section which required both to be played at the same time which will present him with an interesting challenge. Rather than combining the bell and xylophone parts for one player just because they were on the same sheet of music, divide the part between two players. That way the section where both bells and xylophone play together can be played. The bell part is very simple and will be a good one to use for Jim's first attempt at playing bells in the band. The xylophone part is difficult, but quite short, so Sue should be able to do it."

The section leader should always check with the director after determining the assignments and *before* posting them for the other students. In most cases, the director will be able to look at the assignment chart and in a matter of a few minutes, O.K. the assignments. The assignment chart should then be posted in a prominent place in the percussion section so that it can be readily available for reference. It will also help the director if the section leader will make a separate copy of the assignments for the director's folder.

Once the part is assigned, the section leader must be sure that each student has his own copy of each piece. If there are not enough parts available, he should notify the director immediately so that additional parts may be ordered. Each student should mark, *in pencil,* on the top of each sheet the instrument he plays and the equipment he will need for the piece. This would include the number and size, or hardness, of all sticks, special stands or equipment, and any instruments he may have to share with another player during the piece.

Once the music for a concert program is selected, the section leader should make a list of all the percussion equipment needed for that concert. If each player has marked the top of his part as indicated above, the section leader will need only to collect all the parts and copy down the information listed at the top of each sheet. This will enable both of you to know how much equipment will need to be moved, the amount of time that will be required, and the amount of space required in the performance area. If this presents some problems, they can be resolved long before the actual date of the concert.

Your rehearsal can progress much more smoothly if you post the daily rehearsal schedule on the board before each rehearsal. The percussionists can then see which pieces are to be practiced and can prepare their equipment for the day's rehearsal. If you don't do this the percussionists will have to search for the equipment they need each time you announce the next song, causing a great deal of wasted rehearsal time.

Equipping the Percussion Section

Equipment Needs—Following is a list of the basic percussion instruments you will need to equip your section for teaching the total percussion. The instruments are generally listed in the order of importance although specific needs might require your obtaining these instruments in a different order.

1 Bass Drum	16" x 36", wood shell, separate tension, plastic heads. (See Chapter 6, pp. 103-104.)
1 Snare Drum	6½" x 14", metal shell preferred but wood acceptable, plastic heads, wire-wound snares. (See Chapter 5, pp. 85-86.)
1 pr. Hand Cymbals	16" or 17" diameters, medium weight. (See Chapter 6, pp. 107-109.)
1 pr. Timpani	25" & 28" diameters, copper bowls, plastic heads, pedal tuning mechanism. (See Chapter 4, pp. 64-67.)
1 Xylophone	3½ octave range, resonator tubes.
Orchestra Bells	2½ octave range, steel bars.
Marching Percussion	Needs depend upon style and instrumentation desired for marching percussion. (See Chapter 8.)
1 Triangle	10", steel, variety of beater sizes. (See Chapter 6, pp. 112-113.)
1 Woodblock	Large size.
2 Tambourines	8" diameter with single row of jingles and 10" diameter with double row of jingles, wood shell, calfskin head. (See Chapter 6, pp. 115-116.)
1 pr. Maracas	Large size.
1 pr. Claves	Large size.
2 pr. Handle Castanets	Single pair of castanets mounted on each handle.

1 Cowbell	Large size.
1 Suspended Cymbal	16" or 17", medium-heavy weight. (See Chapter 6, pp. 107-109.)
1 Drum Set	Including: bass drum, snare drum, ride cymbal, hi-hat, mounted tom tom and optional floor tom tom. (See Chapter 7, pp. 139-142 for size specifications.)
1 Marimba	4 octave range.
1 pr. Bongos	Adjustable plastic head, stand and adapter.
1 Tam Tam	26" to 30" diameter.
1 Guiro	
1 pr. Concert Castanets	
1pr. Timbales	

The following is a list of additional equipment you will need and should acquire after you have all the instruments listed above. These are listed in order of importance but this may vary depending on your specific needs.

2 Timpani	23" & 32" diameters, copper bowls, plastic heads, pedal tuning mechanism.
Concert Tom Toms	Set of four larger sized tom toms.
1 Set Chimes	1½ octave range, 1¼" or 1½" diameter tubes.
Bell Lyres	Number depends on your marching requirements.
1 Headless Tambourine	Wood shell, any diameter.
1 pr. Hand Cymbals	19" or 20" diameters; medium weight.
1 Suspended Cymbal	21" to 24" diameter, medium or medium-heavy weight.
1 Triangle	6", steel, variety of beater sizes.
1 Woodblock	Small size.

Although not used as often, the following equipment should be purchased when possible to help toward making a completely equipped total percussion section.

Temple Blocks	5 blocks mounted in a single row.
1 Conga Drum	Single drum, with stand and adapter.
1 Vibraphone	3 octave range.
Concert Tom Toms	Set of four drums in smaller sizes.
1 Suspended Cymbal	12" to 14" diameter, thin weight.
1 Triangle	8", steel, variety of beater sizes.
1 Cowbell	Small size.
1 pr. Maracas	Small size.
1 pr. Claves	Small size.

The following are specialty items which should be purchased only when needed as there is a relatively limited need for them.

Antique Cymbals	
Bird Whistle	
Cabaca	
Celeste	Suggest rental of this when needed.
Finger Cymbals	
Ka-Me-So	
Oriental Gong	Suggest rental of this when needed.
Pop Gun	
Ratchet	
Sleighbells	
Siren	
Slapstick	
Slidewhistle	
Tubo	

Instrument Substitutions—Occasionally you will need an instrument you do not have and you may not have the time or money to purchase it. I would advise that you contact surrounding schools and music stores to see if it would be possible to borrow the equipment that you need. If this is not possible there are some substitutions which can be made in emergency situations although they are generally not desirable. Some possibilities are listed below:

Antique Cymbals	Orchestra bells with brass mallet
Bongos	High pitched concert tom toms
Celeste	Orchestra bells with soft mallets
Conga Drum	Large tom tom with yarn mallet
Cowbell	Dome of suspended cymbal
Finger Cymbals	Triangle
Ka-Me-So	Maracas
Slapstick	Snare drum stick against rim of snare drum
Tam Tam	Large, heavy-weight suspended cymbal and heavy yarn mallet
Temple Blocks	Woodblocks with soft-rubber mallet
Timbales	Concert tom toms or two snare drums of different pitches with snares off. Use light stick or rattan shaft of keyboard mallet
Tom Tom	Snare drum or field drum with snares off
Tubo	Maracas
Vibraphone	Orchestra bells in low range with soft mallets
Xylophone	Marimba using hard mallets and playing up one octave

Utilizing a Trap Table—The trap table is one important piece of equipment that every percussion section will need. In fact, it is a good idea to have two or three trap tables available so they can be situated where needed within the section. The trap table can be used for all the small accessory percussion instruments, sticks, beaters and mallets that will be needed. Percussionists need some place to put their small equipment after playing and the chair or floor is not the proper place. By having a well padded table available you can eliminate almost all of the extraneous noises that come from the percussion section during the rehearsal or performance.

Some portable percussion cabinets have tops that double as

trap tables. If the top is not padded (and some are not) glue a piece of carpet to it. These are particularly handy as they have the storage drawers easily accessible. You will still need additional trap tables in your section, however, as one table is usually not enough.

It is also quite easy and inexpensive to make a satisfactory trap table. All that is needed are some two- by three-foot pieces of 3/4 inch plywood and some rug samples or remnant that can be cut to this size. Glue the piece of carpeting to the plywood. Your carpeting store will have a good quality glue and might be willing to do this for the school. Do not nail the carpet down as the exposed nail heads can cause extraneous noises. When the plywood is completed it can rest on a "tray stand" which can be purchased through most restaurant supply catalogs. (Check with your cafeteria supervisor for this catalog.)

Care of the Percussion Equipment

Storage Facilities—Storage facilities for the percussion instruments are used to protect the equipment from damage, keep it clean, organized and easy to find. The director should make a point of instructing his entire group that all percussion equipment is "off limits" to students not in the percussion section as they do not know how to handle the equipment properly. Percussion players should only be allowed to use the equipment during rehearsals and authorized practice times. Unauthorized playing of the percussion equipment along with poor storage facilities can account for almost 90 percent of the percussion damage.

The storage facilities for all percussion instruments should be located immediately adjacent to the percussion section to facilitate the moving of equipment with the minimum of time and effort. This also keeps all the equipment close at hand for access during the rehearsal period. Ideally, storage facilities should contain a number of racks for the larger instruments such as marching percussion, bass drums, snare drums, concert tom toms, etc. Seasonal instruments such as the marching percussion should be in cases and stored on the racks when not in use.

In addition, there should be a combination of shelves and drawers available for storing the smaller and accessory percussion instruments, sticks, beaters, mallets, and slings. There are many commercially made percussion cabinets which can be used for this although it is unlikely many would be large enough to hold all the equipment in the well-equipped percussion section. This cabinet would have to be supplemented, therefore, with additional permanent storage facilities of the same type.

The large percussion instruments such as timpani, marimbas, xylophones, vibraphones, bass drums, etc. should have larger cabinets in which they may be rolled for storage. Sometimes a small room near the percussion section will work well for this. These larger items need not be moved to storage facilities after each use as long as they are covered when not in use. They should be stored, however, whenever they will not be needed for a period of time. Even when in storage these instruments should be covered to keep them free of dust.

All storage facilities should be located away from extremes in temperature, should not be near windows or heating vents, and should have locks so the equipment may be safely secured.

Maintenance—Your percussion equipment should be repaired as soon as you or your section leader notices any damage or wear. In this way the equipment will always be ready for use. Some schools have well-equipped percussion sections, but half the equipment is damaged or in such poor repair that it does not work when needed. Most percussion repairs can be done in the school by the band director. The most common repairs will be the replacement of broken heads or parts which need to be re-ordered but attach without difficulty. Many of the smaller percussion items cannot be repaired but need to be replaced when broken.

In addition to repairing damaged or worn equipment, the director and/or section leader should institute a program of preventive maintenance. By utilizing regular monthly and yearly check-up periods, severe damage can often be prevented. These check-ups should include the following:

The Monthly Check-up

1) Check all drum heads for holes or tearing and replace when needed.
2) Check and replace all sticks and mallets which are cracked, warped or broken.
3) Check and replace or re-cover all mallets and timpani sticks with worn-out heads.
4) Check all snares for loose or broken strands. Cut or replace as necessary.
5) Check all stands for loose wingnuts, screws, etc.
6) Check all accessory percussion instruments for any damage.
7) Wipe all heads with a damp cloth to remove surface dirt.
8) Check all cymbal straps to be sure that knots are secure.
9) Dust bars of all the mallet percussion instruments.
10) Thoroughly tune the timpani. Balance the heads and reset pitches as required.

The Yearly Check-up

1) Remove all heads and clean dirt from inside head, under counter-hoop and edge of shell. Lubricate rim and replace.
2) Remove all gum wrappers, paper clips, etc. that seem to accumulate in drum shells.
3) Clean and lubricate, with Vaseline, all tuning rods.
4) Check timpani for dents while head is off and remove if not too serious.
5) Check all cymbals for cracks. Be sure that all knots are tied correctly.
6) Check the ropes, bumpers and bars of all mallet instruments. Cracked bars and missing bumpers should be replaced.
7) Polish all mallet instruments—wood bars with good quality paste wax and metal bars with good quality metal polish.
8) Check intonation of mallet instruments and send bars to be retuned when needed.

9) Check chime suspension cords for any signs of wear.
10) Check pedal mechanism on vibraphone and chimes for good operation.
11) Reset collars on any calfskin heads which may not be even.
12) Polish and hand buff all cymbals.

In addition to the above general maintenance procedures, there are many references to instrument care within the various chapters of this book. Below is a reference guide to those places:

Chimes	Chapter 3, p. 47
Cymbals	Chapter 6, p. 111
Marimba	Chapter 3, p. 39 (Same as for xylophone)
Orchestra Bells	Chapter 3, p. 42
Snare Drum	Chapter 5, pp. 90-91
Timpani	Chapter 4, p. 67
Vibraphone	Chapter 3, p. 45
Xylophone	Chapter 3, p. 39

Appendix

A Partial Listing of
Percussion Method Books

Listed below is a representative selection of method books for the mallet instruments, timpani, snare drum, drum set and other percussion instruments. This listing is not complete but it is hoped that it will offer the teacher a beginning source of material for teaching the total percussion.

The titles listed are either the more popular methods or those which are relatively recent releases. I have indicated the copyright date for each method and have rated it on a scale of difficulty from elementary to advanced. This scale can be interpreted as follows:

Elementary—for the young student with no previous knowledge of the instrument

Intermediate—either for the student with some knowledge of the instrument or the older beginning student who may progress more rapidly

Advanced—a method which will present a challenge to the *high school* student with a good background on the instrument.

As every book has particular strengths and weaknesses and its own individual approach, I suggest that the teacher review various methods in which he is interested to determine which will best serve his particular needs. Comments about each method are minimal to allow a longer list.

METHOD BOOKS FOR THE MALLET INSTRUMENTS

Elementary
Beginning Duets (2 vols.) by W. Lewis and M. Widner (Adler/Belwin; 1964)

Buggert Method for Xylophone and Marimba by Robert Buggert (Belwin; 1942)

Classical Themes from Bach, Beethoven, Brahms, Vol. I by Harold Farberman (Adler/Belwin; 1966) a collection of progressive duets with optional trio part

Contemporary Marimba Solos, Vol I. by Bobby Christian (Creative Music; 1966) a collection of progressive two-mallet solos

Elementary Method for Marimba and Xylophone by Howard Peterson (Rubank; 1938)

Jazz for Juniors by Carl Pool (Adler/Belwin; 1961) 15 progressive duets designed to develop the interpretation of jazz

Mallet Technique for Bass and Treble Clef (2 vols.) by Saul Feldstein (Adler/Belwin; Vol. I–1964, Vol. II–1967)

A Simple and Practical Method for Xylophone, Marimba and Bells by William Dorn (G. Schirmer; 1950)

Vibes for Beginners by Phil Kraus (Adler/Belwin)

Xylophone and Marimba Method by Florence Schaefer (Adler/Belwin; 1958)

Intermediate

Classical Themes from Bach, Beethoven, Brahms, Vol. II by Harold Farberman (Adler/Belwin; 1966) a collection of progressive duets with optional trio part

The Complete Xylophone and Marimba Method by Duane Thamm (Creative Music; 1966)

Contemporary Marimba Solos, Vol. II by Bobby Christian (Creative Music; 1966) a collection of progressive three-mallet solos

Contemporary Scales and Chords by Rudy F. Hermann (Adler/Belwin; 1962) contains exercises based upon modern chord structure

Develop Sight Reading, Vol. I by Gaston Dufresue and Roger Louis Voisin (Chas. Colin; 1956) a book for any instrument, containing exercises progressing in difficulty and rhythmic complexity

Foundation Studies for Xylophone, Marimba and Vibes by David Gornston (David Gornston)

Intermediate Method for Marimba and Xylophone by Art Joliff (Rubank; 1954)

Jazz for Seniors by Carl Pool (Adler/Belwin; 1963) progressive duets designed to develop the interpretation of jazz

Lesson Plan for Mallet Instruments by George Devens (Adler/Belwin; 1959) exercises based on scales, arpeggios and intervals of all major and minor keys

Mallet Control by George L. Stone (George B. Stone & Son; 1949)

Mallet Technique by Vic Firth (Carl Fischer; 1965) 38 studies without any explanations

Marimba Ensemble Folio by Cornelia Luscomb (Rubank; 1940) a collection of 9 familar songs arranged for marimba quartet using 2 marimbas

Modern Jazz Duets by Dick Hyman (Adler/Belwin; 1956)

Modern Mallet Method, Vols. I & II by Phil Kraus (Adler/Belwin; Vol. I–1958, Vol. II–1959) for two-mallet playing only

Percussion Keyboard Technique by Thomas McMillan (Pro Art; 1962) contains explanations on how to play

Play Vibes by Julius Wechter (Adler/Belwin)

78 Solos for Marimba, Vol. I by Art Joliff (Belwin; 1949)

Xylophone, Vibraharp and Marimba by Emil Sholle (Brook Publishing; 1968)

Intermediate-Advanced

Odd Meter Etudes by Everett Gates (David Gornston; 1962) can be used by any instrument.

Schubert Unaccompanied Song Studies by Willard Musser, Robert Campbell and Sandy Feldstein (Adler/Belwin; 1964) 25 solos for mallet percussion

Advanced

Advanced Duets arranged by Bob Nelson (Chas. Colin; 1952) a collection of duets based upon themes of famous composers

Classical Themes from Bach, Beethoven, Brahms, Vol. III by Harold Farberman (Adler/Belwin; 1966) a collection of progressive duets with option trio part

Contemporary Marimba Solos, Vol. III by Bobby Christian (Creative Music; 1966) a collection of four-mallet solos

Develop Sight Reading, Vol. II by Gaston Dufresue and Roger Louis Voisin (Chas. Colin; 1956) a book for any instrument containing exercises progressing in difficulty and rhythmic complexity

15 Bach Inventions arranged by Morris Lang (Adler/Belwin; 1961) in duet form for all mallet instruments

Four Mallet Studies by Gary Burton (Creative Music; 1968)

Introduction to Jazz Vibes by Gary Burton (Creative Music; 1965)

Jazz Phrasing for Mallets by Johnny Rae (Adler/Belwin; 1961) a supplementary study for the advanced student designed to develop a feeling for playing in the jazz style

Marimba Solo Classics by Howard Peterson (Boston Music Co.; 1953) 9 familiar classical solos with piano accompaniment

Masterworks for the Marimba arranged by Clair Omar Musser (Forster Music Pub.; 1940) a collection of ten Chopin solos with piano accompaniment

Mental and Manual Calisthenics for the Modern Mallet Player by Eldon Bailey (Adler/Belwin; 1963)

Modern Mallet Method, Vol. III by Phil Kraus (Adler/Belwin; 1960) a collection of four mallet studies

Modern School for Xylophone, Marimba and Vibraphone by Morris Goldenberg (Chappell; 1950) a very thorough method which includes many orchestral excerpts

Practical Improvisations by Bob Tilles (Belwin; 1966) stresses improvisation in various keys

Progressive Studies in Double Stops for Mallet Instruments by Albert Payson (Music for Percussion; 1958 & 1967)

Reading and Technical Studies by Billy Dorn (Adler/Belwin; 1962) includes no explanations on how to play; exercises based on scales and arpeggios in various keys

78 Solos for Marimba, Vol. II by Art Joliff (Belwin; 1949)

Style Studies by John Bergano (Music for Percussion; 1969) exercises in modern styles of harmony and notation

Tone-Row Exercises for Mallet Percussion by Howard Zwickler (Music for Percussion; 1967) 14 tone row exercises without any explanation

12 Themes with Jazz Improvisation by Barry Miles (Adler/Belwin; 1963) duets for any instrument

METHOD BOOKS FOR THE TIMPANI

Elementary

Basic Timpani Technic by Thomas McMillan (Pro Art; 1962) 32 full-page exercises using two timpani and progressive use of tuning changes within each exercise

Contemporary Tympani Studies by Eric Remsen (TRY Publishing; 1964)
Elementary Method for Tympani by Harvey S. Whistler (Rubank; 1945)
for two timpani, contains tuning exercises

Intermediate

The Gardner Modern Method for Timpani by Carl E. Gardner (Carl Fischer; 1919 & 1944) explanations somewhat outdated; technical studies for two timpani, orchestral excerpts for two to five timpani, only two pages devoted to pedal timpani and tuning
Ludwig Tympani Instructor by William F. Ludwig, Sr. (Ludwig Drum Co.; 1957) thorough explanations with limited amount of exercise material, no special tuning studies
Timpani Tuning by Mervin Britton (Adler/Belwin; 1967) a supplement designed to develop tuning skills
Tympani Method by Sidney Berg (Belwin; 1953) many exercises and examples of orchestral literature, no tuning changes required within any exercise

Intermediate-Advanced

Classic Overtures for Timpani compiled by Morris Goldenberg (Chappell; 1961) orchestral reproductions
Classic Symphonies for Timpani compiled by Morris Goldenberg (Chappell; 1963) orchestral reproductions
Haskell W. Harr Method for Tympani by Haskell Harr (M.M. Cole Pub.; 1950) contains limited tuning exercises
Romantic Symphonies for Timpani compiled by Morris Goldenberg (Chappel; 1964) orchestral reproductions
Standard Concertos for Timpani compiled by Morris Goldenberg (Chappell; 1969) orchestral reproductions

Advanced

Etudes for Timpani (2 vols.) by Richard Hochrainer (Associated Music Pub.; Vol. I—1958, Vol. II—1967) foreign edition with no explanations
Modern Method for Tympani by Saul Goodman (Mills Music; 1948) divided into four sections: (1) fundamentals; (2) two-drum technique; (3) three- and four-drum technique; (4) repertoire
The Solo Timpanist by Vic Firth (Carl Fischer; 1963) exercises utilizing up to six timpani

Timpani Method by Alfred Friese and Alexander Lepak (Adler/Belwin; 1954) in four parts including: (1) theory; (2) technique; (3) intonation; (4) repertoire

20th Century Orchestral Studies for Timpani by Alan Abel (G. Schirmer; 1970) excerpts from timpani repertoire of the 20th century representing a variety of styles

METHOD BOOKS FOR THE SNARE DRUM

Elementary

Breeze-Easy Method for Drums, Vol. I by John Kinyon (M. Witmark & Sons; 1958) uses rudimental and rhythmic reading approach

Buggert Method for Snare Drum, Vol. I by Robert Buggert (Belwin; 1941)

Class Percussion Method by Thomas McMillan (Pro Art; 1966) includes the playing of snare drum, bass drum, triangle and cymbals

Contemporary Method for the Snare Drum by Thomas McMillan (Boston Music Co.; 1962) rhythmic reading approach used with some study of rudiments

Drum Class Method, Vol. I by Alyn J. Heim (Belwin; 1958) uses the rudimental approach

Drum Method, Vols. I & II by Louis Bellson (Big 3; 1970) probably too easy for high school students

Drum Primer by Louis Bellson (David Gornston; 1966)

Elementary Drum Method by Roy Burns (Belwin; 1962) uses the rhythmic reading approach

Haskell W. Harr Drum Method, Vol. I by Haskell Harr (M.M. Cole Pub.; 1937) uses rudimental approach

The Junior Drummer by Charley Wilcoxon (Charles S. Wilcoxon; 1952) uses rudimental approach

Ludwig Drum Method by William F. Ludwig (Ludwig Drum Co.; 1962) exercises on basic rhythms and counting, rolls introduced near the end, some discussion of other percussion instruments

Mixing Meters by Joel Rothman (J. R. Pub.; 1964) exercises designed for the beginning student which employ mixed time signatures

Progressive Studies for the Snare Drum, Vol. I by Carl E. Gardner (Carl Fischer; 1925)

The School Band Drummer by Harold Prentice (Belwin; 1961) contains basic rhythmic reading and an introduction to some rudiments

7 Rudiments for Beginning Drummer by A. G. Tieman (Pro Art; 1958) uses the right-hand lead system of playing, "Straight System"

The Sturtze Drum Instructor by Earl Sturtze (G. Schirmer; 1955) uses the rudimental approach

The Three R's for Snare Drum (2 vols.) by Acton Ostling (Belwin; 1946)

Intermediate

Advanced Method for Drums by Harvey Whistler (Rubank; 1946) contains some orchestral examples

All American Drummer by Phil Grant (Mercury Music Corp.; 1950) uses rudimental approach

Basic Drum Method by William J. Schinstine and Fred A. Hoey (Southern Music Co.; 1960) uses rudimental approach

Breeze-Easy Method for Drums, Vol. II by John Kinyon (M. Wirmark & Sons; 1959) uses rudimental and rhythmic reading approach

Buggert Method for Snare Drum, Vol. II by Robert Buggert (Belwin; 1941)

Complete Drum Instructor by William F. Ludwig (Ludwig Drum Co.; 1942) uses rudimental approach, contains extensive explanations

Concert Snare Drum by Jack McKenzie (Chas. Colin) uses rhythmic reading approach

Drum Class Method, Vol. II by Alyn J. Heim (Belwin; 1958) uses the rudimental approach

Drum Method, Vol. III by Louis Bellson (Big 3; 1970) probably too easy for high school students; contains some discussion and exercises for the drum set

Drum Warm-ups by Manny Blanc and David Gornston (David Gornston) contains warm-up exercises based on the rudiments; has no explanation on how to play

The Drummer's Heritage compiled by Frederick Fennell (Carl Fischer; 1956) a collection of military music for fife and drum or trumpet and drum (rudimental in style) beginning with Revolutionary War period. Music recorded on Mercury Records, #MG 50111, "The Spirit of '76"

Haskell W. Harr Drum Method, Vol. II by Haskell Harr (M.M. Cole Pub.; 1937) uses rudimental approach

Intermediate Drum Method by Roy Burns and Saul Feldstein (Belwin; 1967) uses rhythmic reading approach with some discussion of rudiments and other percussion instruments

Intermediate Method for Drums by Robert Buggert (Rubank; 1940) uses rudimental approach

Modern Interpretation of Snare Drum Rudiments by Buddy Rich (Embassy Music Corp.; 1942)

Modern Orchestra Drum Technique by Cozy Cole (Mills Music; 1941) uses rudimental approach

Practical Method of Developing Finger Control by Roy Burns and Lewis Malin (Adler/Belwin; 1958) contains some studies on the drum set

Progressive Studies for the Snare Drum, Vol. II by Carl E. Gardner (Carl Fischer; 1926)

Stick Control for the Snare Drummer by George L. Stone (George B. Stone & Sons; 1935 & 1963)

The Straight System by Edward B. Straight (Franks Drum Shop; 1923) exercises designed to develop the system of starting each measure with the right hand

Subject: Control by Marvin Gordon (Alfred Music; 1969) exercises designed to build stick control through the use of accents

Theory Manual of Musical Snare Drumming by D'Artagnan Liagre (TRY Pub.; 1966) designed to teach drum techniques, rhythmic solfeggio and theory. Set up as an 18-week course

Intermediate-Advanced

The All American Drummer by Charley Wilcoxon (Charles S. Wilcoxon; 1945) contains 150 rudimental solos

The Art of Drumming by J. Burns Moore (Ludwig Drum Co.; 1937) uses the rudimental approach

The Big 230 for Snare Drum by Emil Sholle (Brook Pub.; 1968) "short studies for speed and control based on 'rudiments of drumming' "

Drum Method by Charley Wilcoxon (Charles Wilcoxon; 1944) uses rudimental approach and includes bass drum parts to be played with exercises

Fundamental Approach to the Snare Drum by Les Parks (Sam Fox Pub.; 1967) uses rhythmic reading approach

The Moeller Book by Stanford A. Moeller (Ludwig Drum Co.; 1956) uses the rudimental approach

N.A.R.D. Drum Solos collected by the National Association of Rudimental Drummers (Ludwig Drum Co.; 1937 & 1962) collection of short rudimental solos

Odd Time Reading Text by Louis Bellson and Gil Breines (Belwin; 1968)
Progressive Studies for the Snare Drum, Vol. III by Carl E. Gardner (Carl Fischer; 1927)
Reading and Rolling in 6/8 Time by Joel Rothman (Alfred Music Co.; 1967)
Rolls, Rolls, Rolls by Joel Rothman (J.R. Pub.; 1968) exercises utilizing the roll
20th Century Orchestral Snare Drum Studies by Thomas McMillan (Creative Music; 1968) contains exercises utilizing the rhythms of 20th century composers
William F. Ludwig Collection Drum Solos by William F. Ludwig (Ludwig Drum Co.; 1942) a collection of solos in the rudimental style

Advanced

Accents and Rebounds by George L. Stone (George B. Stone & Sons; 1961) designed to follow author's "Stick Control"
Contemporary Studies for the Snare Drum by Fred Albright (Adler/Belwin; 1963)
Drumming Together by William J. Schinstine (Southern Music Co.; 1958) a collection of advanced duets
14 Modern Contest Solos for Snare Drum by John S. Pratt (Belwin; 1959) a collection of rudimental solos
Fun With Triplet By Joel Rothman (J.R. Pub.; 1968) a series of exercises employing the triplet
Gardner Modern Method for the Drums, Cymbals and Accessories by Carl E. Gardner (Carl Fischer; 1919 & 1945) uses rudimental approach
Modern Rudimental Swing Solos by Charley Wilcoxon (Charles Wilcoxon; 1941) rudimental exercises employing syncopated rhythms
Modern School for Snare Drum with a Guide Book for the Artist Percussionist by Morris Goldenberg (Chappell; 1955) first half of book deals with snare drum studies, second half has explanations and orchestral excerpts for most of the other percussion instruments, some multiple percussion solos and percussion ensemble examples included
Musicians Guide to Polyrhythms by Pete Magadini (TRY Pub.; 1967) exercises designed to play two or more different rhythms simultaneously
Odd Meter Rudimental Etudes for the Snare Drum by Mitchell Peters (Mitchell Peters; 1967)
Portraits in Rhythm by Anthony J. Cirone (Belwin; 1968) exercises using mixed and odd-time signatures

Progressive Studies for the Snare Drum, Vol. IV by Carl E. Gardner (Carl Fischer; 1928)

Reading Can Be Odd by Joel Rothman (J.R. Pub.; 1963) contains odd meter exercises

The Solo Snare Drummer by Vic Firth (Carl Fischer; 1968) a collection of etudes without any explanations

Wrist and Finger Stroke Control by Charley Wilcoxon (Charles S. Wilcoxon; 1951) contains sixteenth and triplet rhythms utilizing varying accent patterns

METHOD BOOKS FOR THE DRUM SET

Elementary

Drum Set Primer by Louis Bellson (David Gornston; 1967)

Drum Set Reading Method by Rupert Kettle (Belwin; 1968) "... written to acquaint the student with drum set staff notation and the reading thereof"

Elementary Rock and Roll Drumming by Roy Burns and Howard Halpern (Belwin; 1968)

4 Way Drum Set Method by Buddy McCarthy (Sam Fox Pub.; 1968) develops basic beats for the drum set

Introduction to the Drum Set, Vol. I by Charles Perry (Adler/Belwin; 1958) contains basic patterns using all the instruments of the set

The New Rudiments by Joel Rothman (J.R. Pub.; 1969) contains a series of 94 rhythmic patterns to help develop coordination of the four limbs

A Practical Approach to the Drum Set by John Beck (MCA Music; 1968) develops independence and explains basic jazz, rock and roll, and latin rhythms

Reading With Jazz Interpretation by Joel Rothman (J.R. Pub.; 1964)

Rock Around the Drums by Joel Rothman (J.R. Pub.; 1968) provides easy-to-play drum breaks and solo patterns

Student's Guide to Stage Band Drumming by Chuck Morey and Myron Collins (Kendor Music; 1962)

Talking Drums by Ed Thigpen (Ed Thigpen Prod.; 1965) provides the basic technical studies needed to play jazz

Intermediate

Advanced Rock and Roll Drumming by Roy Burns (Belwin; 1968)

contains elementary exercises for the individual instruments of the drum set and intermediate to advanced examples of varying styles of rock rhythms including fills for each style

Complete Instruction in Dance Drumming by Jake Jerger (Slingerland Drum Co.; 1962) a comprehensive method

Design for Drum Set by Don Lamond (Adler/Belwin; 1957) contains exercises for bass drum and hi-hat (with sticks)

Developing "Drum Breaks" and Fill-ins by Sonny Igoe and Henry Adler (Adler/Belwin; 1959)

Independent Thinking by Joel Rothman (J.R. Pub.; 1966) designed to develop coordination on the drum set

Introduction to the Drum Set, Vol. II by Charles Perry (Adler/Belwin; 1958) contains solos, fills, breaks using various instruments of the set alone or in combination

Modern Jazz Drumming by William F. Ludwig, Jr. (Ludwig Drum Co.; 1958)

Practical Analysis of Independence by Thomas L. Davis (Creative Music; 1966)

Rhythmic Patterns for the Modern Drummer by Joe Cusatis (Belwin; 1963) "full drum set studies including drum-to-drum patterns and cross-sticking patterns"

Rock and Roll Bible of Co-ordination by Joel Rothman (J.R. Pub.; 1968) designed to develop coordination for playing all styles of rock and roll but does not explain the various rock style patterns

Rock-n-Roll-n-Latin Breaks by Joel Rothman (J.R. Pub.; 1965) contains exercises for developing breaks and fills in rock and roll style

Rockin' Bass Drum by John Lombardo and Charles Perry (Alfred Music Co.; 1969) contains exercises of rhythmic patterns to develop coordination for today's rock styles

Sock It To Me by Joel Rothman (J.R. Pub.; 1968) contains studies for the independent use of the hi-hat

Intermediate-Advanced

Cymbal Coordination by Ralph Pace (Drum Book Music; 1969) contains many examples of cymbal rhythms and then exercises maintaining these rhythms to various left hand and foot patterns

Gene Krupa Drum Method by Gene Krupa (Robbins Music Corp.; 1938 & 1966) contains little exercise material, mostly explanations of various patterns; also includes basic study of snare drum and rudiments, progresses rapidly

Modern and Authentic Drum Rhythms by Gene Krupa, Cosy Cole and Wm. V. Kessler (Mills Music; 1958) extensive section on Latin American rhythms

The New Conceptions by Morris Lang (Adler/Belwin; 1965) develops four measure solos utilizing changing meters, uses author's method of writing for the complete drum set

New Directions in Rhythm by Joe Morello (JoMor Pub.; 1963) contains studies in 3/4 and 5/4 jazz

The New Time Signatures of Jazz Drumming by Ed Shaughnessy (Adler/Belwin; 1966)

Practical Percussion Studies by Bob Tilles (Adler/Belwin; 1962) designed to develop independent coordination

Progressive Studies for Double Bass Drums by Louis Bellson (TRY Pub.; 1969)

Rudimental Patterns for the Modern Drummer by Joe Cusatis (Adler/Belwin; 1968) contains drum-to-drum patterns utilizing the full drum set and employing the rudiments

Show Drumming by Irv Greene (J.R. Pub.; 1968) all exercises are examples of hand-written "charts." Student must have some experience in reading such charts as no explanations are provided. Charts are typical of dance band arrangements

The Sounds of Rock and Roll (4 vols.) by Ralph Pace (Drum Book Music; 1969)

Advanced

Advanced Techniques for the Modern Drummer by Jim Chapin (Jim Chapin; 1948) designed to develop independence of each hand and foot

4-way Coordination by Marvin Dahlgren and Elliot Fine (Adler/Belwin; 1963) "a method for developing independence using two hands and two feet"

Rudimental Jazz by Joe Morello (JoMor Pub.; 1967) develops the application of the rudiments to the drum set

METHOD BOOKS FOR THE MARCHING PERCUSSION SECTION

Elementary

Tenor Drum Method by Larry McCormick (Percussion Enterprises; 1965)

Intermediate

The Antiphonal Drum Sectional by A. R. Casavant (Southern Music Co.; 1963) introduces various contrasting rhythms that may be used with the marching percussion section

Back Sticking by Larry McCormick (Percussion Enterprises; 1965) exercises designed to develop the back-sticking technique

Marching Bells by Saul Feldstein and Phil Kraus (Adler/Belwin; 1966)

Tenor, Tenor-Scotch and Scotch Bass Drum Manual by Haskell Harr (Slingerland Drum Co.; 1961) contains cadences and discussion of the marching percussion

Intermediate-Advanced

101 Street Beats by Samuel Floyd (Charles Hansen; 1966) also contains tips on playing and maintenance of the marching percussion

128 Rudimental Street Beats by John S. Pratt (Belwin; 1959) for field drum and tenor drum only

MISCELLANEOUS PERCUSSION METHOD BOOKS

Adler's Percussion Solo Series (3 vols.) by Roy Burns and Saul Feldstein (Alder/Belwin; 1966) Vol. I–Elementary, Vol. II–Intermediate, Vol. III–Advanced; a collection of multiple percussion solos which progress in difficulty through the three volumes. A good introduction to multiple percussion solos

The Art of Playing the Cymbals by Sam Denov (Adler/Belwin; 1963) a reference book with pictures and diagrams of all the phases of playing the cymbals

Authentic Bongo Rhythms by Bob Evans (Adler/Belwin; 1960)

Authentic Conga Rhythms by Bob Evans (Adler/Belwin; 1960)

Bongo Playing Made Easy by Jake Jerger (Slingerland Drum Co.; 1962)

Bongos Made Easy by Chico Arnez (New Sound in Modern Music; 1959) a fully illustrated book on playing the bongos

Latin American Rhythm Instruments and How to Play Them by Humberto Morales (Adler/Belwin; 1954) probably the most complete method on this subject

Learning the Bongos is Easy by Thomas Christie (Wm. J. Smith; 1967)

Let's All Play Bongos by Jack Burger (Robbins Music Corp.; 1958)

Modern Reading Text in 4/4 by Louis Bellson and Gil Breines (Adler/ Belwin; 1963) advanced; designed for any instrument, contains syncopated studies to improve reading skills

Modern School for the Snare Drum with a Guide Book for the Artist Percussionist by Morris Goldenberg (Chappell; 1955) the second part of this book contains descriptions of many of the accessory percussion instruments with orchestral excerpts for each

Playing and Teaching Percussion Instruments by Myron D. Collins and John E. Green (Prentice-Hall, Inc.; 1962)

Reading By Recognition by Joseph Leavitt (Adler/Belwin; 1960) intermediate; designed to help develop reading skills in the percussionist

The Rhythms of Contemporary Music by Joseph Leavitt (Adler/Belwin)

The Selection, Care and Use of Cymbals for the Stage and Dance Band by Roy Burns (Adler/Belwin; 1964) this is a reference book and contains no exercises

Studies in Solo Percussion by Morris Goldenberg (Chappell; 1968) intermediate-advanced; a collection of multiple percussion solos

Techniques and Exercises for Playing Triangles, Tambourines and Castanets by Paul Price (Music for Percussion; 1955) intermediate-advanced

20th Century Orchestra Studies for Percussion by Alan Abel (G. Schirmer; 1970) advanced; contains excerpts from percussion repertoire of the 20th century representing various styles and utilizing different percussion instruments

Index

215

DATE DUE

NOV

6 Oct 15

2 Dec

FEB 1 2 1976

OCT 1 3 1979

OCT 1 6 1990

JAN 0 5 1990

GAYLORD   PRINTED IN U.S.A.

WITHDRAWN